"Wendy's writing always makes me hungry for the Word of God and eager to grow in my love for its Author. *The 40-Day Feast* is such a gift! It will whet your appetite for God Himself as you grow to understand His Word."

Monica Swanson, author of *Boy Mom* and *Raising Amazing*

40-Day Feast Testimonials

"Oh my, what a feast! Wendy Speake delivers again. Each one of her books has blessed my life. (Yes, I've read them all.) I have learned to fill up on Jesus through fasting, and now I'm overflowing as I learn to feast. I absolutely love diving deeper into the Word with Wendy's suggested "Food for Thought" passages. This book truly is a feast for the soul. Wendy has poured out her heart in the pages of this book so that we can find God's heart in the pages of His book!"

Melissa Mathewson

"In this beautifully written devotional, Wendy takes us to the table where our every need is met and our every craving is satisfied. She teaches us to savor God and all His goodness. With every abundant helping, we learn what it is to be filled by God's Word and fueled by His grace so we can become more faith-FULL. Come hungry."

Kay Gleaves

"So much more than a daily devotional, *The 40-Day Feast* is a deep dive into the beautiful Word of God! Written for men and women seeking to go deeper with the Lord every day! If you have a desire to know God better, understand His written Word, and allow it to change how you live, you will love this 40-Day Feast. Expect to find yourself hungrier than ever by the end of this FEAST."

itchel

"After completing several fasts, I was eager to get my hands on Wendy Speake's newest book, *The 40 Day Feast: Taste and See the Goodness of God's Word*. As always, Wendy finds a way to nudge my heart back to what matters most. As she guides us through our own 40-Day Feast, she reminds us of the importance of staying in the Word and increasing our hunger for Scripture, all while giving us practical steps to better engage with the Bible. This is a great resource to believers in all seasons of their faith."

Amanda Gunderson

"I grew up going to church, and I always noticed that no matter how fantastic and spiritually filling the Sunday sermon was, it was never enough to sustain me through the whole week. Before long, I would find myself hungry for more but unsure how to study my Bible. I wanted to learn but had no clue where to start, no matter how many Bible studies I did. Not only did I read this book twice, I also highlighted and put into practice so many things I learned along the way. Every Christian who is struggling to read their Bible—whether they're new in their faith or have been walking with the Lord for years—should grab a copy of this book, then share it with those around them."

Jenn McClure

Praise for *The 40-Day Social Media Fast*

"[This is] a book about much more than social media fasting. If you feel you have lost your way in a noisy world, this book will help you. If you feel overcome by your attachment to the numb of the scroll, in these pages you will find hope.

God has a plan to meet with you—a fresh revelation He wants to speak into your soul. Of that, I am sure. While this fast might at first feel like a tremendous sacrifice on your part, it's really a huge gift from Him."

From the foreword by Lisa Whittle, bestselling author, speaker, podcast host, and ministry coach

"It's almost impossible to be still and hear the voice of God with the relentless hum of technology in the background. I love that this book invites us—in fact, gives us permission—to tune out social media and turn toward the Savior instead for forty days. As you set aside this sacred time, get ready to hear from God and replenish your soul. You won't lose much by ignoring social media posts, but you have much to gain when you seek God!"

Arlene Pellicane, speaker, podcaster, and author of *Screen Kids* and *Calm, Cool, and Connected*

"Our thoughts determine our beliefs, our beliefs determine our attitudes, and our attitudes determine our behaviors, so what we spend time thinking about impacts both how we feel and ultimately how we behave. A decade ago precious little time was spent on the internet; whereas today, social media profiles are growing exponentially and online surfing comprises more of our day than spending time gathered around the table for family meals. *The 40-Day Social Media Fast* is a challenge to all of us to turn from what our behavior proves is our first love (all things online) to the One who desires to be our first and only love. Wendy Speake helps us to see that in and of itself, social media (or food, or music, etc.) is not inherently bad, but when we turn to it to cope rather than to the God with all wisdom, we trade that which will last for eternity for the momentary gratification of a "like," a ping, a calorie, or a tune. If you've found yourself growing disenchanted with life, I'd recommend you read *The 40-Day Social Media Fast*, and intentionally and purposefully re-engage with the One who died to have a relationship with you."

Dr. Michelle Bengtson, board certified clinical neuropsychologist, national and international media resource for mental health and wellness, and award-winning author of *Hope Prevails*, the *Hope Prevails Bible Study*, and *Breaking Anxiety's Grip*

"It's hard for me to overstate how badly we need this book and how badly our families need this book. I long to go to Jesus more than my phone. I long for my children, one day, to go to Jesus more than their phones. We need help to keep technology in its rightful place, and this book is precisely the kind of help we need. Wendy is gracious and humble, and she speaks with authority and kindness. I've always wanted to take a social media break but couldn't get up enough nerve to do it alone. Thanks to this book, I'm not alone. Thank you, Wendy, for blazing the trail as we set the phones down and look to the One who gives true life."

Jessica Smartt, author of *Memory-Making Mom*

Praise for *The 40-Day Sugar Fast*

"Sick of the scale being the boss of me, I needed a different voice in my head. Then I stumbled upon Wendy's 40-Day Sugar Fast, and suddenly the spiritual connection between food, my heart, and God clicked for me. I started to see food as less of a reward or a temptation and more of a means to align my heart back with God's. Food, like all of His good gifts, should always point us back to the Giver. It shouldn't accuse us or guilt us. It should simply remind us what we need to sustain us. This shift in thinking has taken me forty days and beyond. And I'm so grateful for the mental overhaul more than any pounds lost. More than anything I want to be able to say with Jesus, 'My food is to do the will of him who sent me' (John 4:34). And traveling with Wendy and the 40-Day Sugar Fast community was the beginning of that journey for me."

Lisa-Jo Baker, bestselling author of *Never Unfriended* and *Surprised by Motherhood*

"If Wendy is leading, I want to follow. This woman is exceptionally wise with an impressive earnestness for leading people to the feet of Jesus. She is a highly respected mentor and communicator with a passion for pointing people to what matters most. Wendy is much more than a writer who can string a bunch of nice words on the page. Her words bring real results."

"We all want freedom. We want to break free from habits that haunt us, voices that taunt us, chains that bind us, and emotions that blind us. Wendy's onto something huge here! She speaks with depth and authority from the Word of God, and she knows that the emancipation we're all really longing for is actually a person: Jesus. *The 40-Day Sugar Fast* helps each participant experience meaningful growth and lasting peace, as it ushers them to a fresh, personal, and satisfying banquet with the One who longs to be their portion."

"To fast from what we crave in order to find sustaining satisfaction in God is a message for this clamoring culture. And it's a message for me. Wendy's words are for every one of us whose reach for sugar is never enough."

THE 40-DAY

Feast

TASTE AND SEE
THE GOODNESS OF GOD'S WORD

WENDY SPEAKE

BakerBooks

a division of Baker Publishing Group
Grand Rapids, Michigan

Published by Baker Books
a division of Baker Publishing Group
PO Box 6287, Grand Rapids, MI 49516-6287
www.bakerbooks.com

Printed in the United States of America

Library of Congress Cataloging-in-Publication Data
Names: Speake, Wendy, 1974– author.
Title: The 40-day feast : taste and see the goodness of God's word / Wendy Speake.
Other titles: Forty-day feast
Description: Grand Rapids, MI : Baker Books, a division of Baker Publishing Group, [2023] | Includes bibliographical references.
Identifiers: LCCN 2022023119 | ISBN 9781540901255 (paperback) | ISBN 9781540903082 (casebound) | ISBN 9781493439539 (ebook)
Subjects: LCSH: Bible—Appreciation. | Devotional literature. | Bible—Reading. | Bible—Criticism, interpretation, etc.
Classification: LCC BS538.5 .S64 2023 | DDC 220.6—dc23/eng/20220725
LC record available at https://lccn.loc.gov/2022023119

The author is represented by the William K. Jensen Literary Agency.

Baker Publishing Group publications use paper produced from sustainable forestry practices and post-consumer waste whenever possible.

23 24 25 26 27 28 29   7 6 5 4 3 2

Dedicated to the Holy Spirit, who wrote the Word;
to the Father, who wrapped it in flesh and sent it to us;
and to Jesus, who is both the Message and the Messenger!
Be glorified, I pray.

The Bible is not an end in itself, but a means to bring men to an intimate and satisfying knowledge of God, that they may enter into Him, that they may delight in His Presence, may taste and know the inner sweetness of the very God Himself in the core and center of their hearts.

A. W. Tozer, *The Pursuit of God*

Contents

Welcome to the Feast

Taste and see that the LORD is good; blessed is the one who takes refuge in him.

Psalm 34:8

NO BOOK HAS EVER BEEN WRITTEN, nor ever will be, that holds the power to sway a human heart toward the Word of God more than the Bible itself. Yet here I am, setting a literary table and pulling up figurative chairs in an effort to whet your appetite for the written account of God's extravagant, demonstrative, unrelenting love. As I serve up this forty-course feast in the form of daily devotions, it is my hope that you taste the sweetness of God for yourself. Oh, He is good, and His Word is true. Yet many miss out entirely because not all Bible-believing men and women are Bible-reading men and women. As a result, we're a malnourished bunch.

The irony of being spiritually malnourished is that many of us are also overfed on cultural junk food. We are consumers who overeat and overdrink by bingeing shows and social media, online shopping and retail therapy, video gaming and YouTube watching. But none of those things have ever worked to fill our holes and make us whole—or holy. When we turn to food and drink, screens and shopping, to meet our deepest needs, we end up unsatisfied and hungrier than ever. **We are a generation of consumers who never learned to consume God's Word.** We scroll through our phones and scour our cabinets, hungry for something to satisfy, but nothing we find there ever does. We were made for more. We were made for God. And our Bibles are where we find Him.

That is why I spent a year hunkered down over my keyboard, bent over that metaphorical stove, cooking up this feast—not in an effort to feed you for forty days, but to inspire and equip you to feed yourself directly from the bountiful buffet of God's Word. This book will come to an end, but the Word of God never ends (Isa. 40:8). It is the only thing able to satisfy hungry hearts.

Only in our Bibles will we find the help, hope, and healing we're desperate for. In our Bibles we find light for the path we're on and bread for the day ahead. In the pages of God's holy communication, we encounter not only conviction but transformation—and grace. In our Bibles we taste the sweetness of grace, the very goodness of God's redemptive love. As we feast on His forgiveness, we find ourselves forgiven and forgiving. As we open up our Bibles, we discover not only the message but the Messenger—the book but also the Author.

As we read, believe what we read, and confess it with our lips as our own belief, the Holy Spirit, who wrote the Word and dwells in it, lifts off the page and then drops into our hearts like a deposit. He opens our minds to understand that our sins are forgiven, then gives us the strength to stop sinning. It's all there, from Genesis to Revelation. All we have to do is consume it.

Whether or not you are already a Christian, my hope is that after you've spent forty days feasting with me, you'll be hungry for more and confident enough to dig into God's Word on your own. These bite-size devotions aren't meant to satisfy. While I hope this book is good, it is not the Good Book. **This forty-day feast is not a comprehensive explanation of God's Word, but an attempt to make it just a little more comprehensible.** The scope of God's Word is too vast; my abilities to communicate too small; and the facets of God's character revealed within its pages too multifaceted. I failed before I even began, for neither my heart nor my mind can grasp the beauty and majesty of God's communication with humankind—the height is too high and the depth too deep. Still, I did my best to entice you to the table, and now I welcome you to *The 40-Day Feast*.

Let's Get Hungry

The book you hold in your hands contains forty short chapters, one for each day. These readings are designed to whet your appetite for the Word of God. Each one begins with a short verse and ends with a prayer. Afterward, I serve up the *real feast*—a Bible passage for you to read on your own and a thought to chew on. My words are an appetizer; God's Word is the main course.

In the early days of our feast, we will focus our hungry hearts on the sweetness and goodness of God's Word. Together we will consider *what* the Bible is, *who* it is about, *why* we should read it, and *how* it applies to our lives. Many people are confused when they first attempt to read the Bible, but I'm hopeful you will discover that God is a clear and kind communicator. This ancient story is applicable to the story lines of our lives today, for the author is the King of all kings who rules over every generation. God's Word is enduring and endearing, eternal and most loving. Over the course of these forty days, you'll get to taste and see for yourself.

God's Word is enduring and endearing, eternal and most loving.

During the middle section of our feast, you'll learn different ways to study God's Word on your own—*how* to open it up and eat it up without depending on pastors or Bible study leaders to spoon-feed you your faith. I am not suggesting that you forego those guides but consider what a personal time of study and meditation might look like the other six days of the week. Whether you read through one book of the Bible over and over again or start in Genesis and continue through Revelation, you'll discover how to get the most out of God's Word with the help of His Holy Spirit, a few probing questions, and a teachable heart.

Then, as we near the end, when our hearts are finally full and yet hungrier than ever, we will commit to staying hungry. We will commit to staying faithful. We will commit to being unashamed of our biblical worldview in the midst of this dangerously postbiblical age. And above all, we will commit to loving God and loving others as we have been commanded to do. For we do not want to simply feast on the Word, but ultimately do what it says as well.

Perhaps during this feast you will come to cherish your Bible for the first time ever. Or maybe in the early days of your faith you were insatiable, a bona fide Jesus freak who was "on fire for the Lord." Although you once spent great gobs of time in His Word, you've lost your fervor and forgotten its flavor over the years. Either way, I pray these forty days light a fire in your belly. Wherever you are in your faith journey, I invite you to fall head over heels in love with the One who wrote this amazingly applicable book for you as a love letter to communicate how precious you are to Him and how available He is to you.

Pray before You Eat

Perhaps you pray before you eat physical food. Let me encourage you to bow your head before you consume this spiritual feast as well. Make the prayer below your own. Ask God to increase your hunger. For nothing you have ever hungered for, apart from Christ, the One who is the "Word made flesh," has ever worked to satisfy or save. No latte or loved one, no purchase or person, no number on the scale or number of followers online, can give you the sense of purpose or pleasure that Christ provides. And it's all yours for the taking (and the tasting) in the pages of your Bible.

Welcome to the feast!

Oh God, I'm ready to feast. Increase my hunger for You and Your Word. Let me taste Your sweetness and discover for myself just how good You are. I ask this humbly and hungrily, in Jesus's name, Amen.

day 1

AN INVITATION
TO THE TABLE

I am the way and the truth and the life. No one comes to the Father except through me.

John 14:6

FEASTING WAS GOD'S IDEA from the start.

It began in the garden of Eden. Before the Lord made the first man, He made food to sustain him. Fruits and vegetables, grains and legumes, each containing multiplying root systems or self-propagating seeds to keep the feast going and growing from one generation to the next. Fish spawned, swarming in seas; animals roamed the earth, giving birth to their young; and birds filled the sky, nesting and resting long enough to lay eggs and continue the creation cycle so that the feasting cycle might also continue.

God first created the feast and then invited His guests, Adam and Eve. Just as the fruit trees and the creatures were commanded to flourish, God told the man and the woman to be fruitful and multiply so that He would have a continual flow of guests at His all-inclusive table. From the very start, God wanted a relationship with a population of people, the Creator wanted to break bread with the created—feasting in fellowship forever.

> The Garden of Eden, I've come to see,
> Was where God planted the very first feast.
> In the fragrant form of fruit-bearing trees
> Each one embedded with miracle seeds.
>
> From that same garden He spoke this command:
> "Birds fill the sky, and animals the land!"
> The sea filled with fish at the wave of His hand;
> Then God touched the clay and molded a man.
>
> The next thing he did was give man a wife
> And told them to feast for the rest of their life.

I wish this invitation to the table had gone off without a hitch. However, God planted one tree in that garden that was not good for feasting. In fact, He knew that it would absolutely ruin the feast, and that's why He told Adam, clearly and kindly, "You may freely eat the fruit of every tree in the garden—except the tree of the knowledge of good and evil. If you eat its fruit, you are sure to die" (Gen. 2:16–17 NLT). Sometime later, unfortunately, Eve was swayed by a serpent, the deceiving devil himself, when he hissed, "You won't die! . . . God knows that your eyes will be opened as soon as you eat it, and you will be like God, knowing both good and evil" (Gen. 3:4–5 NLT). Enticed by the fruit and the words of the serpent, the woman plucked the forbidden food and ate it. She gave some of the fruit to Adam, and he ate as well.

It was this feast that put an end to the feasting life for which God had created them. In an instant, they knew that they were separated from God's good purpose for them, naked and fully exposed. They felt immediate and great shame. Cowering in the leaves, they hid themselves from God.

I find it both bittersweet and beautiful that He came looking for them right around dinnertime, "the time of the evening breeze" (Gen. 3:8 CJB). Inviting His friends to the table, the Lord called out, "Where are you?"

Adam replied timidly from the brush, "I heard you in the garden, and I was afraid because I was naked; so I hid."

Then the Lord asked a question to which He already knew the answer, "Who told you that you were naked? Have you eaten from the tree that I commanded you not to eat from?" (Gen. 3:8–11).

Adam and Eve confessed the whole truth and God had to follow through with the consequences of their sin. Before He sent them out of the garden of Eden, however, He lovingly made clothes for His friends and dressed them. Then off they went, with the garden locked behind them and a future of labor before them. Eve would labor in childbirth, with great pain, and Adam would labor through toil in the soil, working for the feast that had been so generously provided for him in the garden.

This is why we feast on the Word of God, to understand the love of God.

During these next forty days, I hope to serve up a different sort of meal. Not one at a banquet table, heavy-laden with literal food, but one found in nourishing Bible stories, such as this one about Adam and Eve. As you feast on the Word of God, I pray you discover that the One who created you to feast with Him has also provided a way back to the table.

The consequence of Adam and Eve's sin was a physical separation from God. Unfortunately, we've all experienced the same wayward tendencies and the same sad consequence. But God, in His longing for us, refuses to leave us in our sin and separation. This is the reason Jesus came from heaven to earth, to chase us down and bring us back to the table. He lived the life Adam and Eve couldn't manage to live—and neither can we. Then He took our punishment—the eternal separation our sins deserve—so that we could be forgiven and restored to our place at the table.

This is why we feast on the Word of God, to understand the love of God, shown in the flesh-and-blood person of God, that we might find our way back to God.

The apostle Paul speaks directly of this invitation back to the table:

> Therefore, since we have been justified through faith, we have peace with God through our Lord Jesus Christ, through whom we have gained access by faith into this grace in which we now stand. . . . But the gift is not like the trespass. For if the many died by the trespass of the one man, how much more did God's grace and the gift that came by the grace of the one man, Jesus Christ, overflow to the many! (Rom. 5:1–2, 15)

Sin entered the world through one man, and as a result, humankind was banished from the garden of God's presence and the table where He wanted to fellowship with us. But, praise God, it was also through one man, Jesus, that we have been invited back to that table, that we might enjoy His fellowship again.

That's why it's important to feast on the Bible. We feast on the Word of God in order to understand the way back to God. Jesus spoke this of Himself when He said, "I am the way and the truth and the life. No one comes to the Father except through me" (John 14:6). No one comes back to the table unless invited by the Son. He is the way, this is the truth, and it leads to a forever feasting life with the Father.

Kind Creator, thank You for preparing the original feast—in Your garden and at Your table. Just like Adam and Eve, I tend to push my seat away, willfully and continually. But here You are, wooing me back and showing me the way. Thank You. I pray in the name of Jesus, the One who is the Way, Amen.

THE FEAST

Genesis 1–3

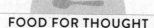

FOOD FOR THOUGHT

As you feasted on Genesis 1–3, in what ways did you taste the tenderness and experience the kindness of our Creator God? Spend some time savoring the sweetness of our Creator's invitation back to the table!

day 2

PRECIOUS MOMENTS

Your words were found, and I ate them,
and your words became to me a joy
and the delight of my heart,
for I am called by your name,
O LORD, God of hosts.

Jeremiah 15:16 ESV

MY FATHER gave me a white, leather-bound Precious Moments Bible when I was young. If you weren't raised in the church in the eighties, you might not know that Precious Moments characters are cartoonlike drawings and porcelain figurines of little children in various poses, always with a Bible verse communicating the main theme of the scene. I had half a dozen of these statuettes atop my bedroom dresser. My Precious Moments Bible was filled with darling pictures, and I loved it with all my little-girl heart.

While the gift was from my dad, who took me to church on Sunday mornings and Wednesday nights, I don't actually have memories of opening that Bible with him. No one in my home taught me to use a highlighter to underline passages that ministered to my heart. I don't recall either of my parents modeling daily Bible reading or serving up God's Word around our family table. Yet somehow I found His words and I ate them, and they became a joy to me and the delight of my young heart. Over the years, I spent many "precious moments" in that Bible.

By the time I was in high school, I had developed a sweet tooth for God's Word. I was drawn to the psalms especially. As a highly sensitive and emotional teen, the poetry of the psalms was a balm to my often-troubled soul. God reminded me through His Word that He was mighty to save, a very present help in my times of trouble, always near and abiding, inclining His ear to me when I cried out to Him. God's Word flooded into the broken places of my heart. I read and experienced that He delighted in me; that He made me, fearfully and wonderfully; and He invited me to take refuge in Him when I felt alone. **Each bitter season, God's Word proved sweet.** I tasted and saw His goodness daily. With what can only be described as childlike faith, I believed.

When it was time for me to head to college, my dad gave me a new Bible. It was a massive Life Application Bible with a red cover. Half of each page provided context and definitions to help me better understand the passages. I remember him joking that it was time for me to have a "big-girl Bible"—and this big-girl Bible was *big*! The day I moved into my dorm room, I sat that hunk of a book on my bedside table. *Thud*. Perhaps it was due to the sheer weight of it, but I grew some spiritual muscle while reading that Bible.

It was during my freshman year of college that I met Lillian Fischer, a campus missionary. Lill was the first person to teach me *how* to study the Word, and then she took it a step further and challenged me to share it. I guess you could say that she taught me how to eat the Word and how to serve it up for others.

I remember sitting with Lill in a café on campus with my great big study Bible on the bistro table between us. Her Bible was there too, but it was small and slender and fit easily into her purse. I noticed how her Bible accompanied her subtly wherever she went, while mine took a forklift to carry with me.

One Friday night I went to a Campus Crusade for Christ event at a college across town. I took the subway, lugging my hefty Bible from stop to stop. Not long after I arrived and settled into my seat, the speaker got up and challenged us to ask God for things that were obviously in line with His character and will—things such as the salvation of our unsaved family members and friends, as well as opportunities to serve others. He then gave us a long stretch of quiet to come boldly and prayerfully before the Lord with our requests. In the silence that night, I asked God for a small Bible, one I could keep close to me wherever I went, so that I could share my faith with others around campus. Since I had just been given a new Bible from my dad and had only a small budget to get me through the school year, I knew it would have to be the Lord providing me with yet another one. So I prayed and I asked.

A Bible that's falling apart represents a life that's been put back together.

The very next day, I went to the campus post office and found a small package in my student mailbox. Wrapped in brown paper with no return address was a petite leather-bound Bible. More than fifteen years would pass before I learned that my uncle Bob had sent it to me.

That was the Bible I carried everywhere during my college years. The Life Application Bible still instructed me each morning, but it was the small, leather-bound mystery Bible that I carried with me throughout my days. Once I graduated, I spent more time with that little Bible. In the hardest season of my young adult life, I took to sleeping with it under my pillow, literally resting my head on the dependability of God's promises and the comfort of His nearness.

Today all three of those Bibles—the Precious Moments Bible, the Life Application Bible, and the petite leather-bound one—are displayed on my bookshelf. Of course, this is not a competition. **The goal isn't to have a Bible collection on your shelf, but a collection of the Bible stored up in yourself.** I merely keep them in plain site as a visual reminder of God's past faithfulness.

Though they are tattered and worn, with bindings falling apart and notes poking out from between thin pages, they are beautiful to me. Throughout my young life, I tended to feel weary and worn myself, which is why I clung to my Bible until it was well-worn. My heart was tender and tattered, so I turned to God's promises with such regularity that those Bible pages became tattered too. God's Word bound me up, and now I have three Bibles coming unbound as a result. The pages are literally falling out of each Bible after falling into my heart over the years.

Nineteenth-century preacher Charles Spurgeon once said, "A Bible that's falling apart usually belongs to someone who isn't."[1] I agree, though I might phrase it this way: A Bible that's falling apart represents a life that's been put back together. Have you come to know this for yourself? Whether you need a new binding on your tattered and torn life or a new binding on your well-worn Bible, I am so glad that you are opening the Word with me today. It is my hope that we have many precious moments together in the days ahead. As you ingest His Word, I pray that it becomes a joy to you and the delight of your heart.

Dear Lord, help me to find Your words and eat them. Let them become the joy of my heart. I pray this in the precious name of Jesus, Amen.

THE FEAST

Psalm 19

FOOD FOR THOUGHT

As you gobble up Psalm 19, notice all the wonderful attributes of God's Word listed in verses 7–11. I pray that you come to taste and see that it's all wonderfully true.

day 3

A CONSPIRACY TO BLESS

Blessed is the one who reads aloud the words of this prophecy,
and blessed are those who hear, and who keep what is written in
it, for the time is near.

Revelation 1:3 ESV

REVELATION IS REGARDED by many as the most confusing
book of the Bible, and yet, within its opening verses we're told
that those who read it, hear it, and keep it are blessed. It's the
only book in the whole Bible that begins with the guarantee that
if we invest time reading it, and allowing it to influence how we
live, we will experience blessing. That blows my mind. Why this
book? Why not the Gospels? Why not the Epistles? Why not the
Old Testament stories that chronicle the lives of God's people,
Israel, and paint a picture of our own wayward tendencies in light
of God's unrelenting love? And why not the whole Bible, for goodness' sake? Why just this confusing last book?

My question, I'm afraid, will remain rhetorical for the time
being. While I'll circle back to consider the book of Revelation at

the end of the chapter, at this point, let's simply believe by faith that God wants to bless our lives through the reading of His Word. Throughout history, many have misunderstood God to be miserly, yet He is generously extravagant when it comes to blessing us. The psalmist declares that "pleasures forever" are found at His right hand (16:11 NASB). God isn't looking to catch us doing wrong so He can punish us. On the contrary, He set us free from the punishment we deserve so He might bless us forever. Everything God does is a generous conspiracy to bless us! And His Word unlocks those blessings.

This begs the question, if God's Word is intended to radically bless us, then what stops us from opening it up and receiving the blessing? I believe there are many reasons why Bible-believing men and women don't actually read their Bibles. Laziness and busyness might make the top of the list, but distractedness and hopelessness are up there too. A lack of tenaciousness and eagerness threaten our faithfulness, leaving us passionless. But the reason I hear most often is that people don't open up their Bibles because of ineptness. They simply don't understand what the Bible is about or how to read it. If you feel helpless, I'd like to offer some help.

Everything God does is a generous conspiracy to bless us!

What you are about to read is a simplified summary of this most extravagant biblical narrative. From Genesis to Revelation, the Bible is a rescue story. As with any good story, there must be a main theme, a setting, and characters. In this case, the main theme is our redemption. The heavens and the earth are our setting, though most of the action takes place on earth. And the main characters are God, His people (Israel), His Son (Jesus), and ultimately all of humanity. It's the story of a Hero-Savior and those in need of saving.

Of course, even the simplest story must also have a plot that includes exposition (backstory), rising action, conflict, a climax, falling action, and a resolution. Within the sixty-six books of the Bible, we find it all. Our backstory begins at the beginning, with the opening line: "In the beginning God created the heavens and the earth" (Gen. 1:1).

Genesis is our exposition. Translated from Hebrew, the word *genesis* means "beginning," and it's where we learn that God existed before all else. It communicates the creation story—how God made the heavens and the earth, created light and darkness from nothingness, separated land from sea and sky from the firmament of earth, then filled it with animals and vegetation. Next, God created a man and a woman in His own image. Two days ago you read the story and learned that God planted the garden of Eden and then planted us in it because He loves us and wants to live with us.

Remember what happened next? The woman ate the one forbidden fruit and then offered it to the man, who ate it too. Adam and Eve were the first to sin, and the consequence of their sin was being thrown out of the garden of Eden. From that point in the story, we begin our rising action toward redemption and reconciliation, for God loved us too much to leave us out of His presence, even when we chose that for ourselves.

The rest of the Bible chronicles God's passionate pursuit. The rising action continues throughout the Old Testament. As long as sin threatens, God woos. He tirelessly provides ways for His people to come back to the table of a restored relationship with Him. Communicated through the voices of the prophets and the words of the law—story after story, chapter after chapter—humankind is given the opportunity to receive or reject the blessing of His rescue. When we choose to reject Him, there are sad consequences, but when we choose to receive Him and repent from our sins, there is immediate forgiveness and restored relationship. All of this is a foreshadowing of the ultimate forgiveness that is coming our way.

When Jesus hits the scene in Matthew, the first book of the New Testament, the pace picks up. As Jesus begins His messianic ministry, a few begin to follow Him, but most of God's people deny Him. Here in the Gospels, we are thrust into the great conflict facing all of humanity—to believe Him or to deny Him. And that propels us powerfully into the greatest climax of all—a climax so transcendent it altered human history and has the power to alter every human heart to this day. Jesus's sacrificial death on the cross and victorious resurrection over sin and separation is the rescue within this rescue story! He snatches us from the pit we deserve and plants our feet on the spacious turf of a right and restored relationship with the Father. What a climax. What a victory.

While it seems as if the story might end there, we each have to accept Christ's invitation to believe and then learn to live differently. Just as the early church believed in Jesus, received His Holy Spirit, and became ambassadors of His message, we have the same call on our lives. We must believe in our hearts that Jesus is Lord and confess with our lips that God raised Him from the dead if we are to experience the Savior's salvation (Rom. 10:9). This is where we receive or refuse the rescue! Once we accept it, the story continues. We must read the letters that were written for our edification and sanctification and then share the message with others. All of this is found in the falling action of our story, throughout the New Testament.

As for the resolution, we find ourselves back at the blessing recorded in the final book of the Bible: "Blessed is the one who reads aloud the words of this prophecy, and blessed are those who hear, and who keep what is written in it, for the time is near" (Rev. 1:3 ESV). The resolution happens when we resolve to live our lives joyfully expectant that our Rescuer will come again for a final victory lap. Though the battle was won on the cross at Calvary, we live in eager anticipation of Christ's triumphant return to earth, when He will establish His kingdom here.

What a rescue. What a story. What a radical conspiracy to bless us by rescuing us from sin and giving us the intimacy and fellowship God intended from the start. Those who believe it's true and, to the very end, live as if His return is imminent are most blessed!

Your Bible may seem elusive at first, but with the help of the Holy Spirit, you will find a clear story, logical instructions for life, and straightforward encouragement that cuts through historical context and meets you in this present moment. God's rescue story is your story. One sweeping epic, one dramatic conspiracy to bless!

Lord God, You are the Rescuer, and I am the rescued. You are the Savior, and I am the saved. Israel's story is my story, and Israel's God my God! Thank You for Your relentless love. In the name of Jesus, the hero of this story, Amen.

THE FEAST

Psalm 18

FOOD FOR THOUGHT

Have you allowed yourself to be rescued? The Bible story is your story! Read it as the ultimate picture of rescue and accept it as your own. If you haven't yet allowed the Lord to reach down from on high and take hold of you, ask Him now to pull you from deep waters, save you, and set you in a spacious place, rescued and redeemed, because He delights in you (Ps. 18:16–19).

day 4

TORAH

Do not think that I have come to abolish the Law or the Prophets;
I have not come to abolish them but to fulfill them.

Matthew 5:17 ESV

GROWING UP in Los Angeles and attending public schools provided me with a diverse community of childhood friends. We spent long weeks together during the summer months, swimming at the local "Plunge" and taking art classes through the parks and rec programs. Regardless of which neighborhood we lived in, how big our house was, what color our skin was, or where we worshiped on the weekends, we were simply kids—kicking balls, riding bikes, and jumping from the high dive. Though I was a Christian, by the time I turned fourteen I had attended half a dozen bar mitzvahs and bat mitzvahs.

A bar mitzvah is the highly celebrated rite of passage for Jewish boys when they turn thirteen, while a bat mitzvah is the coming-of-age equivalent for girls at fourteen. Each celebration begins with a formal ceremony at the local temple where the child has grown up attending Torah school. In Culver City, services were always held at Temple Akiba, less than a mile from my home.

My favorite part of those services was when a temple leader would walk to the back of the sanctuary to retrieve the Torah. In synagogues throughout the world, this sacred scroll is kept at the back of the room within a cabinet called *Aron haKodesh*,[1] or holy ark, in honor of the ark of the testimony, which held the stone tablets upon which God wrote the Ten Commandments.

For thousands of years, as well as on each of those bar mitzvah and bat mitzvah mornings, the doors or curtains of the "ark" were opened, allowing the rabbi or another temple leader to retrieve the Torah and carry it to the front of the meeting hall. Then came the part of the ceremony that has stayed with me all these years—the whole congregation rose to their feet when the Torah was retrieved. In unison, we stood and waited just as the Israelites stood and waited at the base of Mount Sinai when Moses, having been in the radiant presence of God, returned to the valley with God's Words cradled in his arms and his countenance ablaze (Exod. 34).

As a young Christian, I knew that the Torah consisted of the first five books of the Bible: Genesis, Exodus, Leviticus, Numbers, and Deuteronomy. These books are the God-inspired words recorded by Moses for the people of Israel and ultimately for us all. While Christians often refer to these books as the Pentateuch, which means "five books" in Greek, it is the Hebrew name *Torah* that explains God's purpose in giving these books to us. Torah is best translated as "instruction."[2]

As the Torah passed each row, worshipers—men and women, young and old—leaned over one another to touch the ornate scroll. It was a physical stretch, this reaching, but an emotional heart stretch too—a yearning, it seemed to me, to connect with God Himself through His Word. Never in my entire Protestant life had I witnessed such reverence and passion for any portion of God's Word, let alone those first five books.

It was at Temple Akiba, with arms reaching over mine to get to the scroll, that I saw for the first time a tattoo of numbers on the forearm of an elderly woman. Old enough to know my history,

I realized that she was a Holocaust survivor. Decades after her liberation, in one of the back rows of Temple Akiba in Culver City, California, she stretched her weathered arms out to touch the Torah.

When it finally arrived at the front of the room, the rabbi sang these words: "*Barukh attah adonai, elohenu, melekh ha'olam.*" In English, "Blessed are you, O Lord our God, King of the universe." Nearly every person who took the platform for the rest of the ceremony also began with that familiar blessing.

Throughout the service, with whole sections spoken in Hebrew, I began to wonder about the woman sitting next to me, the one whose scent of rose perfume and wintergreen Tic Tacs reminded me of my own grandmother. I wondered how old she was. I wondered if any of her family had survived alongside her. But most of all, I wanted to know how it was that she clung to God during those dark years.

Looking back, I wish I had asked her about her enduring faith and her expressive love for the Torah. I'm reminded of the words of another Holocaust survivor, Corrie ten Boom. Corrie was a Dutch Christian woman who along with her family hid Jews in their home. Eventually the ten Booms were caught by the Nazis and Corrie was sent to Ravensbrück concentration camp. After surviving the war, Corrie wrote, "I've experienced His presence in the deepest hell that man can create. . . . I have tested the promises of the Bible, and believe me, you can count on them."[3]

Had the elderly Jewish woman seated beside me, praying to the "King of the universe," experienced His presence in that "deepest hell that man can create"? While I imagine that God's nearness was her comfort and her strength during the war, the five books that comprise the Torah are only the setup to the rescue story of God's radical, redeeming love. Of course, our Jewish brothers and sisters also have the words of the prophets, the poetry of Psalms, and the wisdom of Proverbs to flesh out the writings of Moses, but they have not yet reached out and taken hold of the rest of the story. They are still waiting for their Messiah; they are still awaiting their rescue.

Throughout their long history, the people of Israel have faced one fierce foe after another. First, the Egyptians held them captive, then almost immediately the Amalekites threatened their newfound freedom on the other side of the Red Sea. Once they entered the land of Canaan, other nations were waiting to war with them. The Hittites, Girgashites, Amorites, Canaanites, Perizzites, Hivites, Jebusites, and perhaps the most famous of the early enemies of Israel, the Philistines.

Then there were the countless crooked rulers within Israel's own kingdom who led the people into sin and rebellion. As a result, God allowed the Babylonians and Assyrians to tear down the nation of Israel and carry its people into captivity once more. Though many returned to Israel after seventy years in exile, the reign of captors didn't end there.

God's Word, from Genesis to Revelation, is the complete revelation of God's rescue story.

Jesus Himself was born under the rule of the Roman Empire. That enemy was so oppressive that all of Israel cried out to God for a radical rescue. They pleaded for their long-awaited Messiah, imagining Him with sword and shield, leading them to victory against their oppressors. But God, in His kindness, offered them a different sort of Savior and a different sort of saving. Instead of a mighty warrior with a slashing saber, God sent His own Son to go to battle against our captor, sin. Jesus came to set every one of us free from the penalties that the law required.

Our Jewish friends know and love the law, but they do not yet know or love the One who fulfilled the law on their behalf—the only One who has the power to forever set them free. Though they are not imprisoned by the Egyptians, Babylonians, Romans, or Nazis today, they have not yet experienced the bondage-breaking rescue Christ came to bring.

God's Word, from Genesis to Revelation, is the complete revelation of God's rescue story. It absolutely begins with the Torah, those five books of instruction, but then goes on to tell of the

Messiah's captive-releasing arrival. That's why, as Christians, we ought to be stretching out our arms and reaching out our hands to touch God's Word with the greatest fervor. And not just to touch it, but to let it touch us. Oh, that we would know this sort of reverence for God's written Word. We have so much more to revere, holding the *complete* revelation of God's redemptive plan in our hands.

"Barukh attah adonai, elohenu, melekh ha'olam." *"Blessed are you, O Lord our God, King of the universe." Thank You for setting the stage for our rescue in the first five books of the Bible. You gave us this holy instruction manual, telling us how to live right and righteous, knowing that we couldn't do it on our own. As did the Israelites before us, we continue to go our own way. But You, O Lord, King of the universe, sent Your Son to rescue us from our self-inflicted captivity! In the name of Jesus, our Messiah, Amen.*

THE FEAST

Psalm 97

FOOD FOR THOUGHT

Did you pick up on the imagery of God as Lord over the universe in Psalm 97? If you read through it without seeing His majesty and power over all heaven and earth, slow down and read it again. Allow your deep reverence for God to blossom into a profound reverence for His Word.

day 5

TRANSFORMING STILL

Do not conform to the pattern of this world, but be transformed by the renewing of your mind. Then you will be able to test and approve what God's will is—his good, pleasing and perfect will.

Romans 12:2

IN 1896 A YOUNG EVANGELIST named Henry Allen Ironside left his position with the Salvation Army in Los Angeles to begin a new outreach ministry in the Bay Area of San Francisco. Though only twenty years old at the time, Henry had been preaching the good news up and down the coast of California since he was a mere sixteen.

One Sunday afternoon while he was out on a walk, Henry heard the familiar brass of the Salvation Army band playing nearby. On the corner of Market and Grant Avenue, he found his old friends ministering to a crowd of over three hundred men and women. When the captain of the group recognized Henry, she asked him to share his testimony.

Among the crowd that day was an educated man who handed Henry his business card after his short message was through. On the front of the card was the man's name, and on the back was this invitation: "Sir, I challenge you to debate with me the question of 'Agnosticism versus Christianity' in the Academy of Science Hall next Sunday afternoon at four o'clock."[1]

After reading the card aloud, Ironside gave both the man and the crowd a compelling response, where he later documented the scene in his memoir, *Random Reminiscences from Fifty Years of Ministry*:

> I am very much interested in this challenge . . . I will be glad to agree to this debate on the following conditions: namely, that in order to prove that Mr.— has something worth fighting for and worth debating about, he will promise to bring with him to the Hall next Sunday two people, whose qualifications I will give in a moment, as proof that agnosticism is of real value in changing human lives and building true character. First, he must promise to bring with him one man who was for years what we commonly call a "down-and-outer." I am not particular as to the exact nature of the sins that had wrecked his life and made him an outcast from society— whether a drunkard, or a criminal of some kind, or a victim of any sensual appetite—but a man who for years was under the power of evil habits from which he could not deliver himself, but who on some occasion entered one of Mr.—s meetings and heard his glorification of agnosticism and denunciations of the Bible and Christianity, and whose heart and mind as he listened to such an address were so deeply stirred that he went away from that meeting saying, "Henceforth, I too am an agnostic!" and as a result of imbibing that particular philosophy he found that a new power had come into his life. The sins he once loved, now he hated, and righteousness and goodness were henceforth the ideals of his life. He is now an entirely new man, a credit to himself and an asset to society—all because he is an agnostic.
>
> Secondly, I would like Mr.— to promise to bring with him one woman . . . who was once a poor, wrecked, characterless outcast, the slave of evil passions, and the victim of man's corrupt living. . . . Perhaps one who had lived . . . on Pacific Street, or in some other

nearby hell-hole, utterly lost, ruined and wretched because of her life of sin. But this woman also entered a hall where Mr.— was loudly proclaiming his agnosticism and ridiculing the message of the Holy Scriptures. As she listened, hope was born in her heart, and she said, "This is just what I need to deliver me from the slavery of sin!" She followed the teaching until she became an intelligent agnostic or infidel. As a result, her whole being revolted against the degradation of the life she had been living. She fled from the den of iniquity where she had been held captive so long; and today, rehabilitated, she has won her way back to an honored position in society and is living a clean, virtuous, happy life—all because she is an agnostic.

Now, Mr.—, . . . if you will promise to bring these two people with you as examples of what agnosticism will do, I will promise to meet you at the Hall at the hour appointed next Sunday, and I will bring with me at the very least one hundred men and women who for years lived in such sinful degradation as I have tried to depict, but who have been gloriously saved through believing the message of the gospel which you ridicule. I will have these men and women with me on the platform as witnesses to the miraculous saving power of Jesus Christ, and as present-day proof of the truth of the Bible.[2]

At that point the captain of the Salvation Army band promised to lead the procession into the hall, playing "Onward Christian Soldiers." The agnostic man quickly brushed them off and walked away.

Nothing else on this earth can transform a sinner to a saint but the power of Jesus at work in a life. I hope that you've experienced such a miracle transformation yourself. Maybe you could have been among the one hundred to accompany Ironside into the hall as a walking, talking billboard of the transforming power of Christ. Perhaps you could have sung the lyrics to the famous hymn, "Amazing Grace," with tears streaming down your face and the whole Salvation Army band backing you up, because you too were once "a wretch," but now you are a beautiful testimony of a life transformed by faith in Christ!

God did a work in our lives, but if we're honest, we all know that we're still works in progress. While salvation is received in a moment, learning to live saved takes a lifetime of moments spent in God's refining Word. The Bible tells us how to be saved, then instructs us how to live saved. This is what it means to be sanctified—set apart as holy and wholly different. Of course, our sanctification doesn't happen naturally, only supernaturally, which is why Jesus boldly prayed to the Father on our behalf, "Sanctify them in the truth; your word is truth" (John 17:17 ESV). God's Word is where our transformation takes place.

The Bible tells us how to be saved, then instructs us how to live saved.

We are not powerless to change when we hold a Bible in our hands, for that Bible holds the power to change us. When we are students of the Bible, we end up with Bible-molded lives. Unfortunately, if we refuse to let the Word shape our lives, the world (and not the Word) will do the job for us. That's why this admonition from the apostle Paul is both an invitation and a warning: "Do not conform to the pattern of this world, but be transformed by the renewing of your mind. Then you will be able to test and approve what God's will is—his good, pleasing and perfect will" (Rom. 12:2).

If you have yet to put your full faith in Jesus Christ for the forgiveness of your sins, it's time to stop running back to those same sin-struggles and learn to walk right. If you have already believed, keep believing and keep leaning into the transforming power of God's Word. Once you've been saved, it's time to work out your salvation! Don't just grow your knowledge of the faith, grow up in your faith.

Pastor D. L. Moody said, "The Bible was not given for our information but for our transformation."[3] The Word tells us how to live, and then, with the indwelling help of the Holy Spirit, *enables us to live it out.* Dear friend, do not settle for being somewhat informed and a little reformed but never transformed. Refuse to remain an infant in your faith—open up the Scriptures and grow up in the faith.

> *Savior, Your Word has the power to both save me and to teach me how to live saved! Sanctify me in the truth. Your Word is truth. I pray in the transforming name of Jesus, Amen.*

THE FEAST

Romans 12

FOOD FOR THOUGHT

As you read Romans 12, did you see how much instruction there is for those of us who have already believed? The purpose of the Bible isn't merely to get us saved but to teach us to live saved in a way that brings great glory to our Savior.

day 6

WHY, NOT HOW

But God demonstrates his own love for us in this: While we were still sinners, Christ died for us.

Romans 5:8

I SLID THE TATER TOTS into the oven as our thirteen-year-old bounded down the stairs. When he saw his dad in the easy chair by the fireplace with a Bible open on his lap, he said, "I already did my Bible reading this morning."

"What did you read?" I asked casually. Asher opened his mouth to answer only to realize that he didn't actually remember. So he closed his mouth, turned on his heel, and darted back up the stairs to retrieve his Bible from his bedside table. A few minutes later, we were seated together at the kitchen counter, the pages of Exodus 22 splayed open between.

"Oh, that's right," he said. "Look, I wrote in the margin, 'God is a God of justice.'"

I asked him to tell me what he meant by that, and my youngest read aloud from his Bible, skipping from one highlighted phrase to the next, "If a man steals an ox . . . he shall repay five oxen for an ox. . . . If a man . . . lets his beast loose and it feeds in another man's field, he shall make restitution from the best in his own field and in his own vineyard" (Exod. 22:1, 5 ESV).

Asher summed it up, "Basically, it's an eye for an eye and a tooth for a tooth. God is strict about consequences. He's all about justice."

"Yes," I said slowly, "God is absolutely all about justice. But He's also totally and completely, 100 percent about mercy and grace." I silently asked God to use His Word to inspire my words as I turned to Romans and read aloud, "But God demonstrates his own love for us in this: While we were still sinners, Christ died for us" (5:8).

Here's the thing about Exodus 22—it's a layup for the gospel. Every law that was given, along with our inability to keep them all, is the stage upon which the redemptive work of Christ plays out. So, while there is justice to be had, consequences to be doled out, and payment due for each wrong done, Christ came and wiped the ledger clean. He paid all the debts we owed for all the sins we committed (and will ever commit) when He demonstrated His love for us by dying on the cross.

While the passage Asher read that morning lays out some good neighborly ground rules for how to treat one another's belongings, it's really about so much more. Every passage, every story, every genealogy, every chapter in every book of the Bible has the power to point our hearts and minds to the redemptive work of Christ.

Asher likes to read through the Bible on his own but readily admits he often doesn't understand it. That's okay. He gets a lot of help from his dad, his Sunday school leaders at church, his trusty commentary, and from me too. I've taught him a few of the Bible study tools that I'll be sharing with you in the chapters ahead. But the first lesson he ever received from me was simply this: "Look for Jesus." Even in Exodus 22, you'll find Him if you're looking for Him.

The Old Testament prophecies point to the New Testament Messiah. The first covenant requires the new covenant, sealed not in the blood of an animal sacrifice but in the blood of Jesus. The

Levitical priests, who interceded on behalf of the people, were but a foreshadow of Jesus, our forever High Priest. The Passover lamb was another picture of Christ, the eternal "Lamb of God, who takes away the sin of the world" (John 1:29). And since we cannot perfectly keep the long list of laws laid out for us in the Old Testament, we need our Savior to perfectly pay the debt for our ongoing list of shortcomings and sins.

Exodus 22 is about more than wandering oxen, trampled vineyards, and broken borrowed tools; it's about the price we must pay for doing wrong, whether on purpose or unknowingly. While these verses revealed to Asher that our God is all about justice, my desire is that Asher discovers in the pages of his Bible that God is also *all about grace*. That's the gospel message, the good news, and it's tucked throughout the Scriptures.

> *It is possible to read the Bible and miss the gospel.*

What I said next to my son is what I want to share with you today. I looked Asher in the eyes and warned, "It is possible to read the Bible and miss the gospel." I heard my husband moan softly in agreement from his chair. Asher turned to his dad, and the two made eye contact. Then our child turned back to Exodus 22 and wrote Romans 5:8 in the margin.

As he jotted down the verse, I remembered the Jesus Storybook Bible we used to read together around the kitchen table when all three of our children were very young. In the pages, author Sally Lloyd-Jones wrote, "Now, some people think the Bible is a book of rules, telling you what you should and shouldn't do. The Bible certainly does have some rules in it. They show you how life works best. But the Bible isn't mainly about you and what you should be doing. It's about God and what he has done."[1]

Before I penned a single word of this book, my dear friend, Bible teacher Asheritah Ciuciu gave me one guiding piece of advice, "Don't teach them how to study the Bible and forget to teach them why." **It is possible to read the Bible and not know the God of the Bible. We must read His words in order to know the One who is the Word.**

That's why we're spending the early days of this feast ingesting our *why* before we even consider *how*. In the process, we'll discover that our *why* is actually a *who*. We read our Bibles to know Jesus—the One who paid our penalties, taking the consequences of our sin upon Himself. Jesus is both the why and the who behind every word, whether written in red or black ink. Pastor James Merritt once wrote, "The primary purpose of reading the Bible is not to know the Bible but to know God."[2]

Every Bible story, every chapter, and every verse points us to Christ. Growing in intimacy with Him through the pages of His correspondence with us is our *why*; Christ is our *who*; and with His help, we will learn *how*.

> *Lord, reveal Yourself to me in the pages of this book so that I know how to look for You in the pages of Your book. I ask this in the name of Jesus, the One I am feasting to find, Amen.*

THE FEAST

John 1

FOOD FOR THOUGHT

You just feasted on one of my favorite chapters in the whole Bible. We will take a deeper look at a couple of verses in John 1 tomorrow, but for now, I hope you catch a vision for (and the flavor of) the Jesus we are feasting to find and ultimately follow.

day 7

THE WORD MADE FLESH

In the beginning was the Word, and the Word was with God, and the Word was God. He was with God in the beginning. Through him all things were made; without him nothing was made that has been made. In him was life, and that life was the light of all mankind. . . . The Word became flesh and made his dwelling among us. We have seen his glory, the glory of the one and only Son, who came from the Father, full of grace and truth.

John 1:1-4, 14

COME RIGHT IN. Pull up a chair. Our first course is already on the table. We're looking at two Greek words today so that we can apply the right one to our reading. As you reread the passage above, notice the repetition of "the Word." In verses 1 and 14 alone, "the Word" is mentioned four times. Apparently God wants us to savor its meaning, so let's consider what it means.

In English, we have one word for the term *word*. However, in Greek, there are two words—*rhēma* and *logos*—and each has a slightly different meaning.[1] *Rhēma* typically refers to a specific spoken statement. For example, when the angel appeared to Mary and told her that she would conceive and give birth to God's Son, Mary responded, "Behold, I am the servant of the Lord; let it be to me according to your word [*rhēma*]" (Luke 1:38 ESV). But *rhēma* is not the word John used to refer to Jesus in John 1.

Instead, the word that is repeated four times in this short passage is *logos*. *Logos* doesn't refer to a short statement, but a complete message. Therefore, we might better understand the meaning of "the Word" in our passage of study by reading the verses this way: "In the beginning was [the complete message of God], and [the complete message] was with God, and [the complete message] was God. . . . [That complete message of God] became flesh and made his dwelling among us."

God put flesh on His message and then sent it to us in the form of a Messenger so that we might hear the message, see the message, touch the message, and receive the complete message. Ultimately, there's nothing more important to God than us getting *this message*.

We study the Word to know the One who is the Word.

In one of the most well-known Bible verses, we're told, "For God so loved the world that he gave his one and only Son, that whoever believes in him shall not perish but have eternal life" (John 3:16). God wrapped the complete message of His love for humanity in flesh, so that He might send His message—Jesus—into our midst, to dwell with us and invite us back into a right relationship with the Father forever. A living love letter, God with us.

Incredible.

When Jesus came to earth, fulfilling the word [*rhēma*] spoken by the angel of God to Mary, the complete message of God [*logos*] took human form in her womb. For thirty years, Jesus grew in wisdom and stature and favor with God and humans (Luke 2:52). But finally, in Luke 4, we find the full-grown Messenger, ready to share the complete message that He was born to bring. The chapter begins with Jesus being led by the Holy Spirit out into the desert to be tempted by the devil for forty days. During that time Satan attempted to distract Jesus from His calling, but Jesus fought back by speaking verses from the Torah. The Word was wielding the Word. The Word made flesh used the written Word like a sword to battle back the Enemy.

After that battle of words, Jesus came out of the desert season *well-seasoned*, ready to fulfill His complete purpose. The next story we read is of Jesus, walking into his hometown of Nazareth. It was the Sabbath, so he went to the synagogue. Here's what happened when He stood up to read the Scriptures.

> The scroll of the prophet Isaiah was handed to him. Unrolling it, he found the place where it is written:
>
>> "The Spirit of the Lord is on me,
>>> because he has anointed me
>>> to proclaim good news to the poor.
>> He has sent me to proclaim freedom for the prisoners
>>> and recovery of sight for the blind,
>> to set the oppressed free,
>>> to proclaim the year of the Lord's favor."
>
> Then he rolled up the scroll, gave it back to the attendant, and sat down. The eyes of everyone in the synagogue were fastened on him. He began by saying to them, "Today this scripture is fulfilled in your hearing."
> All spoke well of him and were amazed at the gracious words [*logos*] that came from his lips. (Luke 4:17–22)

Interestingly, the people were not impressed by his *short statements*, but by His *complete message*. And the same thing happened when he spoke in Capernaum. When Jesus was in the synagogue there, the people were "amazed at his teaching, because his words [*logos*] had authority" (Luke 4:32).

On day 5, I encouraged you to consider *why* you should study the Bible before diving into *how* to do it. Let me say it again this way: We study the Word to know the One who is the Word. We uncover the message as we spend time with the Messenger. Jesus is both—the message and the Messenger. He is the Word made flesh.

In Revelation 19:11–13, we are told in no uncertain terms that Jesus truly is the Word of God! However, it's more than a description of what He does; it is actually His name.

> Then I saw heaven opened, and behold, a white horse! The one sitting on it is called Faithful and True, and in righteousness he judges and makes war. His eyes are like a flame of fire, and on his head are many diadems, and he has a name written that no one knows but himself. He is clothed in a robe dipped in blood, and the name by which he is called is The Word of God." (ESV)

What a thrill! When Jesus was creating the world, He was referred to as "the Word" (John 1:1). When He came to earth the first time, He was called "the Word made flesh" (John 1:14). And when He returns again, He will be known as "the Word of God" (Rev. 19:13).

Jesus, You are, You will be, and You always have been, "the Word of God." You are the complete message of God—with skin on. Tender my heart to You as I read Your Word. Jesus, Logos, it is in Your name I pray, Amen.

THE FEAST

Luke 4

FOOD FOR THOUGHT

Luke 4 closes with this emphatic statement from the One who is *the Word made flesh*: "I must proclaim the good news of the kingdom of God to the other towns also, because that is why I was sent"

(v. 43). Jesus was sent to bring *you* the good news! If you were the only person in a town, He would have walked there. Goodness, if you were the only person on earth, He would have come! How does that resonate in your heart?

The more I am able to comprehend the extent that Jesus went to in order to bring the message of God's redemptive plan to me, the more I want to see that message taken to the farthest corners of the world today!

Just as Jesus, the Word made flesh, traveled from town to town, the good news continues to spread all around the world through Bible translation. And you can be part of that! The Seed Company is actively involved in Bible translation today!

A portion of the proceeds from the sale of this book will be given directly to the Seed Company to enable the ongoing translation and distribution of the good news. To learn more and to join me in supporting the Seed Company, visit www.seed company.com.

day 8

BIBLE WOUNDS

He sent out his word and healed them.

Psalm 107:20

MY EARLIEST MEMORIES of being taught from the Bible are of Ruth Gosting. Her flannel board stories were the building blocks of my young faith. Ruth was the director of the children's ministry at Bel Air Presbyterian Church in the late seventies and early eighties. She stocked the children's library with short stories we could check out and take home. For every book we read she put a check mark in her personal ledger. When we hit some magic number, she rewarded us with scratch and sniff stickers, rainbow erasers, and other fantastic prizes.

On Sunday mornings we played games, sang the books of the Bible, and listened to her stories. Ruth had an animated, high-pitched voice that was full of inflection and wonder. To this day I can recall the sound of her singing, "Zacchaeus was a wee little man, and a wee little man was he." Her eyes were always wide open, as if she were perpetually surprised, and every time she saw me, she exclaimed, "Oh, Wendy, I'm so glad you're here!" And she was. And so was I.

I loved church because I was loved at church. And the people who loved me well loved their Bibles too. I wonder if that has anything to do with the tender affection I had for my own Bible as a young girl. I've heard it said that people don't care how much you know until they know how much you care. My heart was wide open to receive Ruth's words because her arms were wide open to receive me, Sunday after Sunday.

Were you loved well by the Bible-believing people in your life? Did you go to church and experience a sincere love there? Was the Bible read at the breakfast table by your mom or dad, your grandma or grandpa? Did they patiently help you apply it to your life in a gracious way? Or did legalistic leaders at church and a fear-based religion at home negatively impact your view of God and His Word? I've heard many people say that they simply never felt welcome, whether in the children's ministry or in "big church," so they stopped showing up and never opened their Bible again.

If you had a negative experience with those who claimed to love God but didn't love you, I'm sorry. Perhaps, as a result, you have "Bible wounds." Unfortunately, in the hands of humanity, God's Word has sometimes been used as a club to beat people rather than a balm to bring them healing. Today, I want to invite you to let the Word, which may have undone your heart in the hands of others, be the instrument God uses to bind your heart up again.

God's desire has always been to bind up and heal broken hearts (Ps. 147:3). We're told that the Lord is near to the brokenhearted (Ps. 34:18). And when Jesus stood up in the synagogue and read from the scroll of Isaiah, He took this job description as His own when He said, "The Spirit of the LORD is upon Me . . . He has sent Me to heal the brokenhearted (Luke 4:18 NKJV).

Many within our churches and around the world have broken hearts, broken relationships with others, and a broken relationship with God. Men and women are held captive by age-old wounds. Today, let's invite God to do His job—to bring healing to our lives.

Charles Spurgeon once preached, "There are many sorts of broken hearts, and Christ is good at healing them all."[1] Jesus came to bind up your broken heart and repair your broken-down relationship with the Father, and He uses His Word to accomplish the healing and bring about the binding. The psalmist affirms, "He sent out his word and healed them" (Ps. 107:20).

Jesus's wounds have the power to heal our wounds.

Some heart wounds are deeper, harder to perceive, and much more difficult to heal than physical abrasions. Cuts to the heart require the tenderness of a God who knows our frailties and cares about our humanity. Jesus, who is fully God, was also fully man, and He can identify with us in our afflictions. All of them. Jesus hears us when we cry out, "Be merciful to me, O LORD, for I am frail; heal me, O LORD, for my bones are in agony (Ps. 6:2 BSB). He understands our pain because He, too, was physically and emotionally battered and bruised.

However, His pain went a step further. Jesus's pain didn't simply enable Him to identify with us in ours; His affliction was ultimately the means God used to heal us from our afflictions.

> [Jesus] was pierced for our transgressions,
> he was crushed for our iniquities;
> the punishment that brought us peace was on him,
> and by his wounds we are healed. (Isa. 53:5)

Jesus's wounds have the power to heal our wounds. There's a lot to unpack there, but I want to encourage you to ingest the thought of it, meditate on His healing Word, and ask His Holy Spirit to lead you to a place of healing and wholeness. If your parents, peers, or pastors wounded you over the years, bring those deep cuts to Jesus.

It is my hope that during this gospel feast, God uses these Scriptures as a balm to bring healing to your heart. I wish we could sit together in a Sunday school class, in little plastic chairs, and sing some of the old songs with a childlike faith. Just as Ruth said countless times to me, I would say to you, "I am so glad you're here." And then we'd sing another round of her favorite song:

> Zacchaeus was a wee little man
> And a wee little man was he.
> He climbed up in a sycamore tree
> For the Lord he wanted to see.
> And when the Savior passed that way
> He looked up in the tree,
> And said, "Zacchaeus, you come down!
> For I'm going to your house today!"[2]

After singing these words, Ruth would put the tree on her flannel board, then place little Zacchaeus high up in the branches and use her animated voice to tell the story again. She would remind us that even though we were little, we were big to Jesus. Today I want to invite the child in you to believe the same is true. Even if you never visited a church in your youth and only learned about the Lord later in life, the invitation remains. Jesus sees you, He knows you, He wants to come to your house and feast with you because, like Ruth, He is so glad you're here.

Jesus, thank You for preaching the gospel to my heart today. You came to heal it. I believe that's true. Restore my childlike faith, and help me to forgive those who have hurt me within the church, within my home, and over the course of my life. While Your Word brings healing, forgiveness is a balm too. I pray in the healing name of Jesus, Amen.

THE FEAST

Psalm 147

FOOD FOR THOUGHT

I once met a woman who said, "I want to go to heaven, I just don't want to have to spend eternity with a bunch of Christians." (Sigh.) Church is complicated. As a matter of fact, all families are. But church can be the most complicated of all because there are so many family members living in the house of God.

Each and every person the world over is a sinner—Christians are merely sinners who have been saved by grace. Unfortunately, we still struggle with sin. Christian churches and Christian homes are full of imperfect people seeking to know a perfect God. The transformation process can be slow and arduous, and along the way, Christians often hurt other Christians. Sometimes offenses are overt and obvious, other times they are merely mistakes and misunderstandings. Either way, the pain is real. Invite God to bring healing to your heart, your memories, and your life today. Take Him at His Word: He came to bind you up, and He uses His Word to do just that!

day 9

THE BOOK THAT UNDERSTANDS ME

You have searched me, LORD, and you know me.

Psalm 139:1

BORN IN DAMPIERRE, FRANCE, on December 17, 1894, Emile Cailliet was raised in a home where the Bible was not read. His education focused on the natural world with no mention of the One who made it. As a matter of fact, young Cailliet never even saw a Bible until he was twenty-three years old.

When Cailliet went off to war, a war started in his own heart, a battle to know and be known in a way he never had before. He later wrote, "During long night watches in the foxholes [in WWI] I had in a strange way been longing—I must say it, however queer it may sound—for a book that would understand me. But I knew of no such book."[1] Though he was well-read, he had never read anything that helped him understand life or feel understood in his life. And so, when he was later wounded in the war and released from the army, he made the plan to compile such a book—a book that would understand him thoroughly.[2]

As he read from the great authors of literature and philosophy, Emile Cailliet jotted down quotes in a leather-bound journal. He copied whole passages that attempted to ask the same questions he himself had. Once his book of quotes was completed, he sat down beneath a tree to read it through. Unfortunately Emile experienced even deeper despair for he still lacked what he longed for. He didn't understand and certainly did not feel understood by this book, so he tucked it down deep in his pocket.

At that very moment, Emile's wife came to him with a gift. Knowing nothing of her husband's quest or the book he had compiled, she placed a Bible in his hands and shared a story that surprised them both. Earlier that day, she had been out for a walk in their small village. When she came upon a little Huguenot chapel, she found herself walking in and asking for a Bible. She was shocked by the request that came from her mouth, knowing that her husband looked down on the Christian faith. But when Emile reached for it, he displayed no arrogance, only eagerness. He later wrote:

> I opened it and "chanced" upon the Beatitudes [Matthew 5]! I read, and read. . . . I could not find words to express my awe and wonder. And suddenly the realization dawned upon me: This *was* the Book that would understand me! I needed it so much, yet, unaware, I had attempted to write my own—in vain. I continued to read deeply into the night, mostly from the gospels. And lo and behold, as I looked through them, the One of whom they spoke, the One who spoke and acted in them, became alive to me. . . .
>
> The providential circumstances amid which the Book had found me now made it clear that while it seemed absurd to speak of a book understanding a man, this could be said of the Bible because its pages were animated by the Presence of the Living God and the Power of His mighty acts. To this God I prayed that night, and the God who answered *was the same God* of whom it was spoken in the Book.[3]

Many people never read the Bible because they were not raised in a Bible-reading home. And yet, innately, deep in the fiber of their being, they long to know and be known by its Author. Today I want to suggest something radical: The Bible is not something we seek to understand, but a book we open because it understands us. It knows our history and our humanity, our striving and our suffering, our joys and jubilation, our DNA, depression, doubts, and dreams. The living and active Word understands and applies to our flesh and our family, it speaks into our sin-struggles and soul-sadness, and it shines its light on our past and bears testimony to a bright future ahead.

The Bible is not something we seek to understand, but a book we open because it understands us.

The Bible is the only book that understands you so intimately that your whole life will begin to make sense through its lens. Before you ever crack the cover and read one word, the One who is the Word is reading you. He knows you and understands you, for He made you.

God tells us that we are to love Him because He loved us first (1 John 4:19). Likewise, we begin to understand Him because we're so intimately understood. If you have struggled to comprehend the Bible, let the fact that God knows you propel you into a life of knowing Him. He knows your hopes and dreams as well as your abilities and inabilities. He never takes His eyes off you. Even when you feel lost and alone in the darkest night, in the trenches of your own soul's war, even then He is with you, for the darkness is as light to Him (Ps. 139:12). Such knowledge is too wonderful for us to comprehend.

Oh, to be loved like that. Oh, to be known. Oh, to be understood. Therefore, because He loves you, love Him back. Because He knows you, know Him. Because He understands you, understand Him. God reads you like an open book, so open up His book and read Him back!

Lord, Your love for me is more than I can comprehend. Your knowledge of me is too wonderful! Help me to remember that the next time I am tempted to stop reading my Bible because I don't understand it. Because You know me so intimately, I want to know You back. Reveal Yourself to me. I ask humbly and expectantly, in Jesus's name, Amen.

THE FEAST

Psalm 139

FOOD FOR THOUGHT

Even if the Bible sometimes confuses you, quietly consider that God isn't confused one bit about who you are or what you need today. How might you respond to this idea that He intimately understands you and loves you? Might I suggest you invite Him to help you understand Him back? The more time you spend in His presence and in His Word, the easier such knowing and being known will become.

day 10

BITTERSWEET

"Son of man, eat this scroll I am giving you and fill your stomach with it." So I ate it, and it tasted as sweet as honey in my mouth.

Ezekiel 3:3

IN MY JEWELRY BOX are small tokens of love, given to me mostly by my husband and my mother over the years. I value them greatly and wear them regularly. But within that box is something I prize most of all; not a pendant of gold, but something much more valuable. The torn and partially eaten corner of a thin Bible page.

When my firstborn child was only a few months old, he was rolling around and batting at toys, and I sat beside him, reading my Bible on the living room floor. Without warning, my baby boy rolled onto his side, stretched out his chubby hand, and ripped out part of the page I was reading. In one fluid motion, he shoved it into his slobbery mouth. Quickly, I reached in after it, pulled it out, wiped it off, and attempted to flatten it. Eighteen years later, that torn Bible page is taped to the inside of my jewelry box, and it is more valuable than anything else in residence beside it. No rubies, diamonds, or gold can compare.

Speaking of gold, before my son ate that page, I had used a golden highlighter to mark these words: "Turn to me and have mercy on me; show your strength in behalf of your servant; save me, because I serve you just as my mother did" (Ps. 86:16). How beautiful the irony. As a young mom, most likely tired from too many sleepless nights, I was pleading for God's strength and asking for salvation for my child. Of all the pages and all the prayers, this was what my baby grabbed and ate.

To share the story with you now is special. I haven't shared it in written or spoken words before. But here we are, considering how we might figuratively feast on God's Word for forty days and well beyond. I pray that my infant son's literal example inspires us greatly.

Long before baby Caleb put that Bible page in his little mouth, God instructed others to eat His words. The prophet Jeremiah said, "Your words were found, and I ate them, and your words became to me a joy and the delight of my heart, for I am called by your name, O LORD, God of hosts" (15:16 ESV).

In the book of Ezekiel, we find another scroll-eating prophet, living in the land of the Babylonians. Both Jeremiah and Ezekiel were God's mouthpieces during a long, hard season of exile for His people. The Israelites had disobeyed God's law for centuries and abandoned their faith each time they grew comfortable in their prosperity. As a consequence, God sent an enemy army to uproot them and run them out of Canaan, the promised land. During that painful season of discipline, the Lord sent a vision to Ezekiel as he sat beside the Kebar River.

The Lord spoke directly to Ezekiel, "Son of man, eat what is before you, eat this scroll; then go and speak to the people of Israel" (3:1). In his vision, Ezekiel saw a scroll being extended to Him. The Lord repeated, "Son of man, eat this scroll I am giving you and fill your stomach with it" (v. 3). When Ezekiel took the scroll and ate it, he discovered that it tasted as sweet as honey. Perhaps you're reminded of the Psalm you read on day 2, which confirmed that God's Word is in fact "sweeter than honey, than honey from the honeycomb" (19:10).

There is yet another man in the Bible who had an experience similar to those of Jeremiah and Ezekiel tasting the sweetness of God's Word. The apostle John was exiled on the island of Patmos in Greece when God sent him a vision, clearly instructing him through an angel, "Go, take the scroll. . . . Take it and eat it. It will turn your stomach sour, but 'in your mouth it will be as sweet as honey'" (Rev. 10:8–9). Sure enough, when John took the scroll from the angel's hand and ate it, it tasted sweet like honey. Once he had eaten it, however, his stomach turned sour. Then John was told, "You must prophesy again about many peoples, nations, languages and kings" (v. 11).

Jeremiah, Ezekiel, and John were all told to eat God's words in order to prepare them to share God's words with others. How kind of the Lord to allow His Word to bring joy and a delight to Jeremiah's heart and a surpassing sweetness to Ezekiel's taste buds. John, too, tasted the sweetness when he had eaten the scroll. Unfortunately, its sweet message held a bitter taste for those who refused it. *Belief enables our spiritual taste buds.* The Israelites didn't want to hear God's message through the prophets, and John's message about the Messiah was offensive to those who denied Christ. We are told in 1 Corinthians 1:18 that "the message of the cross is foolishness to those who are perishing, but to us who are being saved it is the power of God." **The message of salvation is always sweet for those who believe but bitter for those who refuse to believe.**

I find it interesting that all three of these men were in exile when their visions and invitations to eat God's Word came to them. All three delighted in the taste of God's holy communication. All three were then told to communicate the sweet message with others. And the messages of all three were bitterly denied to varying degrees in various ways.

As I come to the end of this appetizer-like devotional and send you into the feast that is God's Word, I encourage you to receive the Bible as the sweet communication it is. Ingest it, not with your mouth, but with your heart. Eat it up with your eyes and your mind. And digest it as you actively believe it to be true. Believers receive truth as a sweet gift, while unbelievers find it bitterly offensive. Belief enables our spiritual taste buds.

We will consider the call to share God's Word with unbelievers when we near the end of our feasting days. For now, I simply want to invite you to grab hold of the Word of God through faith in Him. Even if you are an infant in your faith, follow the example of my infant son, and shove the Word into your mouth.

> *Lord God, some people love Your Word and others do not. Some people find it sweet and others bitter. Help me experience Your sweetness as I seek You in Your Word. I humbly and hungrily pray, Amen.*

THE FEAST

John 11:1–44

FOOD FOR THOUGHT

Based on what you read in John 11, how would you describe the sweetness of belief in contrast with the bitter sorrow of unbelief? For those who do not yet believe, there is weeping and wailing beside the grave. But for those who believe, the sweetest hope is offered through the resurrection power of Jesus Christ.

day 11

OUR DAILY BREAD

Give us this day our daily bread.

Matthew 6:11 ESV

SOME OF MY EARLIEST MEMORIES include my grandparents, Jeanette and George Speake. Whether we were up at their cabin in the mountains or down at their apartment in the city, Grandma and Grandpa were an important part of my growing up years. Honestly, I could write a whole book on the legacy they left behind, but today I'll merely tell the story of Grandma's breadbasket.

Meals with Grandma and Grandpa were always special. Though Grandma wasn't a particularly good cook, she excelled at serving those canned Pillsbury biscuits that fall apart in buttery layers. At meals, there were always *two* breadbaskets on the table. One held the biscuits and the other a stack of thin paper napkins topped with a small devotional book. The name on the cover was *Daily Light*, though, even as a child, I thought it should have been called *Daily Bread*. After all, Grandpa would pick it up out of a literal breadbasket.

When Matt and I married in 2001, acquiring a copy of the *Daily Light* devotional was important to me. I had witnessed the longevity of my grandparents' marriage and knew that the foundation of its success was that biblical bedrock. What a gift it was when author Anne Graham Lotz created an updated edition of that same devotional. Not long after we married, I purchased a copy at a bookshop near our first home, where Anne herself was signing copies.

But the story of *Daily Light*'s original publication begins in 1772, when Samuel Bagster was born in England. Brought up in a Bible-believing home, he was educated in the faith and then worked as an apprentice to a bookseller. In 1794 he opened his own bookshop in London. Only twenty-one years old at the time, young Samuel committed to never sell books that might contradict his faith or lead readers astray.

A few years later Samuel married Eunice Birch, and together they had twelve children. Their tenth child, Jonathan, was the one who came up with the idea for a book, originally titled *Daily Light on the Daily Path*. By that time, Jonathan was a husband and father himself and prepared daily readings for his own family. As editor-in-chief of the family business, he decided to publish *Daily Light* for others to enjoy as well. Although his daughter Anne was his main assistant, it was his son Robert, Samuel Bagster's grandson, who eventually published the collection of 732 morning and evening readings in 1875.[1]

While I love that story, there's a Bible story that best captures what it looks like to eat the bread that God provides each day. In Exodus 16 we discover the nation of Israel right after Moses led them out of captivity in Egypt. After passing through the sea on dry ground, the people arrive in a desert. It didn't take long for them to start grumbling, "If only we had died by the LORD's hand in Egypt! There we sat around pots of meat and ate all the food we wanted, but you have brought us out into this desert to starve this entire assembly to death" (v. 3).

But the Lord was patient with His complaining kids and generous too. He rained down "bread from heaven" each morning for them. This bread descended like dew on the ground. When the dew was gone, thin flakes like frost remained on the desert floor. When the Israelites saw it, they did not know what it was. *Manna* is the word they used to describe this heavenly bread, and it translates literally from Hebrew as, "What is it?"

> Moses said to them, "It is the bread the Lord has given you to eat. This is what the Lord has commanded: 'Everyone is to gather as much as they need. Take an omer for each person you have in your tent.'"
>
> The Israelites did as they were told; some gathered much, some little. And when they measured it by the omer, the one who gathered much did not have too much, and the one who gathered little did not have too little. Everyone had gathered just as much as they needed. (vv. 15–17).

Later, Moses would recap the story this way:

> [God] humbled you and let you hunger and fed you with manna, which you did not know, nor did your fathers know, that he might make you know that man does not live by bread alone, but man lives by every word that comes from the mouth of the Lord. (Deut. 8:3 ESV)

Perhaps you recognize the end of the verse, for these were the words Jesus used to fight Satan in a desert season of His own, when He was tempted, weary from hunger: "It is written: 'Man shall not live on bread alone, but on every word that comes from the mouth of God'" (Matt. 4:4).

Later, when Jesus taught His disciples to pray, He reminded them of their need for daily bread. Not manna, but a different sort of sustenance—the Word of God (Matt. 6:11).

Morning and evening, my grandparents read the Word aloud together at the table. Afterward, Grandpa would pray, then he'd lean over the table and kiss Grandma. Every single day, this was their routine, morning and evening.

Many people consume the Bible like it's cake to be eaten on special occasions, but it is our daily bread. You must go out and gather it daily, like manna. God has sent it, but you still must go and get it. When you read it, you reap it.

Many people consume the Bible like it's cake to be eaten on special occasions, but it is our daily bread.

As you commit to a daily habit of Bible study, think about leaving your Bible on the kitchen table as a reminder to eat it up, then prayerfully consider feasting on the Scriptures more than once a day. Your body gets hungry and needs nourishment multiple times throughout the day—your spirit does too.

Dear Lord, thank You for sending me daily bread. I understand that I need to take an active role in gathering it and feasting on it. May I grow to hunger for it like never before. I pray in the name of Jesus, the Bread of Life. Amen.

THE FEAST

John 6:25–59

FOOD FOR THOUGHT

Today's feast tells the story of when Jesus called Himself the Bread of Life. Many who heard Him that day were confused, and perhaps you are too. But something beautiful happens when we read and reread our Bibles—these single-serving stories start working together to help us understand the complete feast that is our Bible. Consider reading and rereading your Bible, morning and evening, to understand the words of the One who is our daily bread.

day 12

THY WORD

Your word is a lamp for my feet, a light on my path.

Psalm 119:105

IN 1984 AMY GRANT released a song she cowrote with her friend and fellow recording artist, Michael W. Smith. Michael had set to music Psalm 119:105 from the King James, "Thy word is a lamp unto my feet, and a light unto my path." Amy loved it and immediately agreed to write the two short verses.[1] "Thy Word" became one of the biggest contemporary Christian songs of my generation, and as a result, many of us have this short verse embedded deep in our hearts and minds today. Unfortunately, while we might sing that it's true, too few of us live like it is. We don't use the lamplight of God's Word as it was intended. We turn the switch on and off when we want to, then wonder why we're stumbling in the dark yet again.

Recently, I've witnessed a loved one struggle with the consequences of continually disobeying God's Word. Though he believes it, he refuses to allow it to light his path. As a direct result, he keeps tripping over God's clear and kind commands and finding himself face down in the darkness, face down in the mud—over and over again. As I look on from the sidelines, the word *disobedience* comes to mind.

It takes obedience to actively open our Bibles, but it requires even greater obedience to remain in the light day after day— walking in the light and living in it. We must continually allow God's Word to counsel and guide us down the right and righteous road that is well lit. If we don't, we will find ourselves in the dark once again.

It is possible to read your Bible and hear God say one thing, then choose to live however you want. For example, here's what God's Word tells us about lying:

"Do not tell lies about others." (Exod. 20:16 CEV)

"The LORD detests lying lips, but he delights in people who are trustworthy." (Prov. 12:22)

"If you want to enjoy life and see many happy days, keep your tongue from speaking evil and your lips from telling lies." (1 Pet. 3:10 NLT)

If you struggle with telling the truth, you can read all the verses about lying, but you still have to choose whether or not to obey them. You must yield to the counsel that you read in the light in order to walk it out in the light.

Similarly, you may struggle with sexual sin and feel the conviction of God's Spirit as you read the apostle Paul's admonition, "For this is the will of God, your sanctification: that you abstain from sexual immorality; that each one of you know how to control his own body in holiness and honor" (1 Thess. 4:3–4 ESV). Believing the words are true is one thing. It's another thing altogether to allow this light-bright command to propel you down the well-lit path where you actively choose to obey.

Jesus said, "I am the light of the world," and then invited us to walk in the light with Him: "Whoever follows me will never walk in darkness, but will have the light of life" (John 8:12).

My feasting friend, taste the promise above: When we walk with Jesus, we never walk in darkness, but we have the light of life! His presence casts a circle of light upon our path, but the circle is not wide because He doesn't want us to wander. He keeps it tight so that we stay tight, close by His side. He loves us tremendously and helps us to find our way as we remain close by His side, under the lamplight of His Word.

Jesus said, "I have come into the world as a light, so that no one who believes in me should stay in darkness" (John 12:46). This is a clear call to not only believe what you learn in the light but to remain in the light as you walk it out by His side.

Yesterday we witnessed how God provided the Israelites with the perfect amount of bread (manna) every day they wandered in the desert. All they had to do was gather it up each morning. If they did, they would be fed. **Just as God generously provides just enough bread for the day ahead, He also offers us just enough light for the step we're on.** But we have to keep the light on by keeping our Bibles open. And then we need to take it one step further and obey: do what He tells us to do, go where He tells us to go, and behave in a manner that is right and good. We are to obey what His Word makes blindingly clear.

You must yield to the counsel that you read in the light in order to walk it out in the light.

Long before Amy and Michael released "Thy Word," another duo of songwriters wrote the hymn "When We Walk with the Lord," which is more commonly known as "Trust and Obey." In 1886 music composer Daniel B. Towner was leading worship for one of Dwight L. Moody's revivals when a man in the crowd responded to the gospel message, "I am not quite sure—but I am going to trust, and I am going to obey." Towner wrote down the man's words and sent them to his friend, a Presbyterian minister named J. H. Sammis. It was Reverend Sammis who wrote the lyrics, and the hymn was published the following year.[2]

We opened today's devotion with this psalm-song: "Your Word is a lamp for my feet, a light on my path" (Ps. 119:105). Now I would like to wrap it all up by inviting you not only to trust that the Bible is true but to obey what you find there.

> When we walk with the Lord
> in the light of His Word,
> what a glory He sheds on our way!
> While we do His good will,
> He abides with us still,
> and with all who will trust and obey.[3]

Jesus, You are the Light of the world and Your Word is the lamp-light I need. Help me to not only believe that Your Word is true but to live like it's true. Fumbling in the dark and landing in the mud is no longer an option for me. I'm ready for the light! I'm ready to trust and obey. In Jesus's name, Amen.

THE FEAST

After you read Psalm 119:105–112 in your Bible, read it again as theologian Eugene Peterson phrased it in The Message:

> By your words I can see where I'm going;
>   they throw a beam of light on my dark path.
> I've committed myself and I'll never turn back
>   from living by your righteous order.
> Everything's falling apart on me, GOD;
>   put me together again with your Word.
> Adorn me with your finest sayings, GOD;
>   teach me your holy rules.
> My life is as close as my own hands,
>   but I don't forget what you have revealed.
> The wicked do their best to throw me off track,
>   but I don't swerve an inch from your course.

I inherited your book on living; it's mine forever—
    what a gift! And how happy it makes me!
I concentrate on doing exactly what you say—
    I always have and always will.

FOOD FOR THOUGHT

I love the way Eugene Peterson interpreted Psalm 119. I'm also inspired by the way he summed up Jesus's invitation: "I am the world's Light. No one who follows me stumbles around in the darkness. I provide plenty of light to live in" (John 8:12).

In what ways are you living in the illuminating pool of light that Christ provides? In what ways might you be living in the darkness just beyond?

day 13

THIRSTY

As a deer pants for flowing streams,
so pants my soul for you, O God.

Psalm 42:1 ESV

IN 1981 MARTIN NYSTROM, a music teacher in Seattle, Washington, hit a dry spell in his spiritual life. During summer break that year, Martin traveled to Dallas to attend Christ for the Nations Institute. It was there that Martin's roommate suggested he go on a fast to rediscover his joy in the Lord.

On day 19, Martin was seated at a piano on campus, fiddling with a simple chord progression, when he noticed a Bible on a music stand nearby. The Bible was open to Psalm 42. As soon as Martin read the opening verse, he sang a loose translation of the Scripture along with the melody he had been playing. Immediately inspired, the rest of the short song tumbled out. Within minutes, a song he never intended to write was finished.[1]

When you open your Bible to Psalm 42, you will read this notation: "For the director of music. A *maskil* of the Sons of Korah."

The New English Translation renders the Hebrew word *maskil*, as "a well-written song." I love how the original well-written song inspired Martin Nystrom's *maskil*, which I grew up singing as a child—and sang often throughout the writing of this book.

We know that Martin Nystrom was in a dark, dry, depressed season when he wrote his psalm-inspired song. The words he read resonated in his heart, then flowed effortlessly out over his lips:

> As the deer panteth for the water
> so my soul longeth after Thee.[2]

The particulars of Martin's heartache aren't important, for we all have heartaches, but I do wonder what it was that inspired the sons of Korah to thirst for God with such intensity. This Hebrew boy band must have been in a spiritually dry season themselves to write of such longing for God.

While I don't know the particulars of what these men were going through at the time they wrote Psalm 42, I do know that during dry desert seasons, our thirst for God and His Word increases unlike any other time in our lives.

The sons of Korah also wrote Psalm 84, and you can hear the continued longing in this line: "My soul yearns, even faints, for the courts of the LORD; my heart and my flesh cry out for the living God" (v. 2).

If you are in a barren season right now and find yourself longing for God, hungry for His Word, and desperate for His fellowship, I want to suggest with tender sensitivity that you are blessed. Though we would all prefer to avoid pain and suffering, depression and soul-sadness, those who have thirsted to the point of death and experienced the refreshing living water of God's Spirit (to the point of new life) are most blessed. To come to the place where nothing you can purchase with money is able to satisfy your soul's deep thirst is the doorway into true satisfaction.

Here's the invitation God spoke through Isaiah and extends even today to those who are parched for His presence:

> Come, everyone who thirsts,
> come to the waters;
> and he who has no money,
> come, buy and eat!
> Come, buy wine and milk
> without money and without price.
> Why do you spend your money for that which is not bread,
> and your labor for that which does not satisfy?
> Listen diligently to me, and eat what is good,
> and delight yourselves in rich food. (55:1–2 ESV)

Whether you are in a sudden season of soul-sadness (famished for God's faithfulness and thirsty for His refreshing) or you have been thirsty your whole life (but never known where to turn), this promise is for you! God satisfies as nothing else can. Nothing you buy with money can do the trick, for the refreshing that God offers through Christ is already paid for. That's why His refreshing is both free and freeing!

God refreshes weary men and revives worn-out women. He mends broken hearts and feeds all who are famished, that we might literally sing aloud our gladness and our joy. With the psalmist, we invite God to "satisfy us in the morning with your unfailing love, that we may sing for joy and be glad all our days" (Ps. 90:14).

The comfort of His filling brings life to our bones and joy to our hearts.

Since I know the radical refreshing of God firsthand, it is my joy to extend the cup to those who are weary from thirst in a dry desert season of their own. Of course, we all need God, but if you are wasting away, famished and faint, pitifully parched and painfully aware of your need for a good long drink of His refreshing, this one is for you.

Longing feels like aching, but longing is a gift. A deep soul thirst may be uncomfortable, but the comfort of His filling brings life to our bones and joy to our hearts. Hunger causes deep pain—we call those hunger pangs—but when that pain drives us to consume the satisfying reality of God's presence found in His Word, then we are finally feasting!

If your hurts have caused you to reach out to God, then praise Him for the hurt! If your thirst has caused you to finally accept the life-giving waters, then splash in the coolness of His never-ending springs. And if you are already thirsty but long to become thirstier still, then end this devotion with me by praying this prayer by A. W. Tozer:

> *O God, I have tasted Thy goodness, and it has both satisfied me and made me thirsty for more. I am painfully conscious of my need for further grace. I am ashamed of my lack of desire. O God, the Triune God, I want to want Thee; I long to be filled with longing; I thirst to be made more thirsty still. Show me Thy glory, I pray Thee, that so I may know Thee indeed. Begin in mercy a new work within me. Say to my soul, "Rise up, my love, my fair one, and come away." Then give me grace to rise and follow Thee up from this misty lowland where I have wandered so long.*[3]
> *In the satisfying name of Jesus, Amen.*

THE FEAST

Psalm 63

FOOD FOR THOUGHT

Do you long for God and His refreshing Word as one who longs for water in a dry land? Notice how King David praises God in the midst of his thirst, because God has satisfied him before! Spend some time praising God for His past faithfulness as you anticipate the refreshing that is coming your way. Drink up and praise Him!

day 14

DRY BONES

"The days are coming," declares the Sovereign LORD,
    "when I will send a famine through the land—
not a famine of food or a thirst for water,
    but a famine of hearing the words of the LORD.
People will stagger from sea to sea
    and wander from north to east,
searching for the word of the LORD,
    but they will not find it.

In that day
    "the lovely young women and strong young men
    will faint because of thirst."

Amos 8:11–13

TODAY WE'LL CONTINUE to consider our hunger and our thirst for God's Word. Though we've already explored how God uses dry desert seasons and spiritual soul-sadness to draw us to His life-giving water, there is yet another reason we might experience spiritual dryness.

In the Old Testament book of Amos, we're told that God sent a famine upon the land of Israel. Not a famine of literal food or water, but of God's Word. He allowed multiple generations to live through an empty era without hearing from Him. Why would He do such a thing? Why would He refuse to speak to His people? It was, I'm sad to say, because His people had grown obstinate and refused to listen and obey. The Hebrew nations of Israel and Judah were not honoring the words God spoke to them through His prophets and judges, so He stopped speaking until they grew hungry for the sound of His voice again.

God uses dry spiritual seasons to awaken in us a deep thirst for His Word.

Just as we all grow hungry and thirsty without food or drink, God uses dry spiritual seasons to awaken in us a deep thirst for His Word. He allows us to get to the place where we cry out as the psalmist did, "I lie in the dust; revive me by your word" (Ps. 119:25 NLT). Unlike the Israelites of old, we have the whole of God's Word with us today. **God is always speaking, but we refuse to listen when we refuse to read.** In His long-suffering, ongoing kindness, He uses each one of our self-imposed Bible famines to bring us to the place where we are finally famished!

I can look back over my life and see the times I stopped feasting. I stopped reading and therefore stopped listening. God used each wayward season to increase my hunger and bring me back to Him, often malnourished.

Perhaps you've been in and out of Bible seasons too. Sometimes feasting on an abundance of truth, other times finding yourself too busy. Out of habit, you form new habits. In lieu of opening your Bible, you open your phone. Instead of taking your weary heart to His refreshing Word that offers rest and renewed strength, you take it to a glass of wine to revive your heart again. Such habits form quickly. I'm sad to say that I speak from experience, but I've also experienced the return journey home to the heart of God and to the Word of God.

With the psalmist we confess, "I lie in the dust; revive me by your word."

Whether you are feasting with me and find yourself turning to God for the first time or you are in need of returning for the umpteenth time, God's invitation remains the same: "Return to me and I will return to you!"

One of the last prophets through whom God spoke before going silent for four hundred years was Zechariah, whose ministry dated from 520–515 BC. It was through Zechariah that the Lord spoke these words:

> "Return to me," declares the LORD Almighty, "and I will return to you," says the LORD Almighty. Do not be like your ancestors, to whom the earlier prophets proclaimed: This is what the LORD Almighty says: "Turn from your evil ways and your evil practices." But they would not listen or pay attention to me, declares the LORD. Where are your ancestors now? And the prophets, do they live forever? But did not my words and my decrees, which I commanded my servants the prophets, overtake your ancestors?
>
> "Then they repented and said, 'The LORD Almighty has done to us what our ways and practices deserve, just as he determined to do.'" (1:3–6)

Though God may look like a harsh, punitive master, read the passage again and note how the cry of His heart is restored fellowship with His people. He always extends an invitation, "Return to me and I will return to you."

If you are in a dry season and feel the dryness down to your bones, whether it is because you have turned from God or never turned to Him at all, consider the words God spoke through the prophet Ezekiel fifty years before Zechariah became God's mouthpiece:

> The hand of the LORD was upon me, and he brought me out in the Spirit of the LORD and set me down in the middle of the valley; it was full of bones. And he led me around among them, and behold, there were very many on the surface of the valley, and behold, they

were very dry. And he said to me, "Son of man, can these bones live?" And I answered, "O Lord God, you know." Then he said to me, "Prophesy over these bones, and say to them, O dry bones, hear the word of the Lord. Thus says the Lord God to these bones: Behold, I will cause breath to enter you, and you shall live. And I will lay sinews upon you, and will cause flesh to come upon you, and cover you with skin, and put breath in you, and you shall live, and you shall know that I am the Lord." (37:1–6 ESV)

Today I join with Ezekiel to prophesy over your bones. If you have ears to hear, then hear the word of the Lord and believe that He is speaking to you: "Thus says the Lord God to [your] bones: Behold, I will cause breath to enter you, and you shall live. And I will lay sinews upon you, and will cause flesh to come upon you, and cover you with skin, and put breath in you, and you shall live, and you shall know that I am the Lord."

I also join with the prophet Isaiah to give you this promise: "The Lord will guide you continually and satisfy your desire in scorched places and make your bones strong; and you shall be like a watered garden, like a spring of water, whose waters do not fail" (58:11 ESV).

If you are in a desert season, that doesn't mean you've been deserted. God promises, "Never will I leave you; never will I forsake you" (Heb. 13:5). If you're feeling abandoned, in a dry and lonely place, it must be you who did the leaving. God doesn't leave, which means the solution is an easy one—return.

That said, perhaps you have not wandered from God, but still His Word feels dry in this season. That happens too. Seventeenth-century writer and preacher John Bunyan once wrote, "I have sometimes seen more in a line of the Bible than I could well tell how to stand under, and yet at another time the whole Bible hath been to me as dry as a stick."[1]

If that's where you find yourself today, not in need of turning or returning but in need of God stirring and restirring His Word within your heart, He can do that too! And what a wonderful request to make of Him.

God, here I am, listening to Your Word and responding. Turning and returning. Bring Your Word to life in me, and in so doing, bring me back to life! I pray all this in the life-renewing name of Jesus, Amen.

THE FEAST

Isaiah 43

FOOD FOR THOUGHT

If you have been in a dry season where God's Word seems dry and God Himself unresponsive, jot down Isaiah 43:18–19 on a notecard and tuck it in your pocket and into your heart today.

day 15

A FIRM FOUNDATION

The grass withers and the flowers fall,
but the word of our God endures forever.

Isaiah 40:8

MY HUSBAND, MATT, AND I had a very short, long-distance courtship before getting engaged. I loved the Lord, he loved the Lord, and we laughed at the same jokes. What more did we need? And so, after only a few months, we were married on a sandy shore in Redondo Beach, California. I walked the aisle, shoeless, in a traditional wedding dress. My mom made blue wraparound skirts for my bridesmaids, and we found sleeveless white blouses to finish the simple outfits.

The ladies were lovely! And the men were handsome in their linen pants and dress shirts with daisies pinned to their lapels. Everything was simple, including the flowers. Blue delphinium dressed the arbor under which Matt and I said our vows, and then the flowers were carried inside to decorate our dining table.

Our closest family and friends were with us on the beach that day as surfers cheered from the waves beyond us. The weather was perfect, and our love was big. Our pastor read Isaiah 40:8 aloud during the ceremony. It was our wedding verse and remains our marriage verse to this day, reminding us to look to God's Word for all we need to deal with our daily struggles and endure life's storms together. Anything else, everything else—from the world's wisdom to the strong pull of our own emotions—will fail us terribly. Those things are temporary and unstable, shifting like sand each time a new tide rushes in, but the Word of God is steady and sure—and able to keep us steady and sure.

The Word of God is steady and sure—and able to keep us steady and sure.

Perhaps you know the story Jesus shared of the wise man who built his house upon the rock. When the winds rose up and the rain pounded down, the house stood firm upon its foundation—unshaken within and without. Sadly the foolish man didn't follow suit. He built his house and his hopes, his family and his fortune, upon a sandy shoreline. When the wind picked up and the rain came down, his house came down with it (Matt. 7:24–29).

While Matt and I were married on the sand, we committed to building our marriage upon the rock of our salvation, the unchanging Word of God. When the rainy seasons come (in the form of financial stress, health challenges, parenting pressures, and unending busyness) and strong winds blow (with unkind words, selfish choices, and hurt feelings), we know where to take a stand and find our answers. God's Word is not shifting, therefore it holds the power to shift us back on course as it reminds us how to live and how to love and how to endure.

Whether we are married or single, the invitation to build our life upon the forever-foundation of a biblical bedrock is extended to us all. We must build our lives upon that which is eternally true rather than currently comfortable. **Truth, God's truth, is rock-solid and unchanging.**

The psalmist proclaims, "Forever, O Lord, your word is firmly fixed in the heavens" (119:89 ESV). How lovely a thought that God's Word is not only beneath our feet but above our heads. When the wind blows our emotions and our circumstances all about and we feel disturbingly wind-tossed and shaken, we must believe what is eternally true, rather than go along with our present feelings or our culture's shortsighted opinions.

Long ago, reformer Martin Luther wrote this poem:

> For feelings come and feelings go,
> And feelings are deceiving;
> My warrant is the Word of God,
> Naught else is worth believing.

> Though all my heart should feel condemned
> For want of some sweet token,
> There is One greater than my heart
> Whose Word cannot be broken.

> I'll trust in God's unchanging Word
> Till soul and body sever:
> For, though all things shall pass away,
> His Word shall stand forever![1]

You may be in the middle of a storm right now. Perhaps you're facing a torrential downpour in your marriage, or maybe a flash flood is flowing through your family, sweeping you off course, along with your children. Oh, I can relate to that. Truly, I can.

Just the other day, my husband and I hopped on a video call with our family therapist to help us through some very present struggles with one of our teenagers. We needed counsel—biblical counsel. Before the session started, I reached for the large study Bible beside me on the desk and slipped it under the laptop. My desire was to elevate the computer screen, that we might all see eye to eye. However, the metaphor of setting my computer upon the firm foundation of God's Word was an even bigger benefit. Because my husband and I, along with our therapist, are Bible-believing, committed Christians, we were indeed able to see eye to eye.

Twenty years ago, when Matt and I said "I do" on that sandy beach, I had no idea how hard some of our married life would be. I am grateful beyond words for the Word. It has proven a stabilizing ground beneath us.

Discovering what is true in God's Word and fixing your mind upon it will give you clarity about how to stand firm and give you the courage to keep on standing. The apostle Paul reminds us, "Whatever is true, whatever is noble, whatever is right, whatever is pure, whatever is lovely, whatever is admirable—if anything is excellent or praiseworthy—think about such things" (Phil. 4:8).

When Jesus compared the wise man to the foolish man in Matthew 7, He said that we are wise when we hear His Word and obey it. Likewise, we are foolish when we do not hear or do what He says. Let's commit to being wise men and women who hear the Word of God and think about it regularly, then obediently do what it says—build our lives upon the rock. When the rains fall, the floods come, and the winds begin to blow and beat upon the walls of our lives, we will not fall. For though the grass withers and the flowers fall, God's Word remains both firm beneath our feet and fixed forever in the heavens above (Isa. 40:8).

Lord, You are the rock of my salvation and the firm foundation upon which I stand. Shifting sand isn't where I want to be. Thank You for teaching me to build my house upon the guidebook You've so generously written and given to Your children. Help me to fix my mind on what is true and keep my feet firmly planted there. Convict me where I'm slipping and show me in Your Word how to move those areas of my life onto the bedrock of Your plans and purposes. In the rock-solid name of Jesus I pray, Amen.

THE FEAST

1 Peter 1

Matthew 7:24–27

FOOD FOR THOUGHT

Pinpoint one stormy area of your life in this present season, then consider what God's Word has to say about it. If there is a broken relationship, search for Bible verses that teach you how to be reconciled. If you are emotionally unstable, look for stabilizing truths.

Allow God's eternal Word to speak into the temporary circumstances you are experiencing now. That's how we stand upon the rock when the winds blow and the rains come.

Let me encourage you to download the free topical study guide found at wendyspeake.com/feast. Find a subject there that resonates with you and allow God's Word to speak truth into your present reality. Feast upon the Scriptures regarding parenting or perseverance, marriage, depression, or anxiety. Whatever your hardships may be, there are Scriptures that speak into those stormy struggles.

day 16

DID YOU COME TO HEAR FROM THE LORD?

Call to me and I will answer you, and will tell you great and hidden things that you have not known.

Jeremiah 33:3 ESV

FOR TEN YEARS I sat under the Bible teaching of Dennis Keating, the pastor of our local church. Before opening the Word each Sunday morning, our pastor would grasp the podium with both hands, look out into the congregation, and ask this simple, pointed question: "Did you come to hear from the Lord today?" After a moment of silence in which we all quietly answered him in our hearts, Pastor Dennis would pray, inviting the Lord to speak to us through His Word. Then and only then would we open our Bibles together and turn to the passage we were studying that morning.

So here are a few questions for you:

- Do you ask God to open the Scriptures to you before you open them up yourself?

- Do you open God's Word expecting Him to speak directly to your heart and into your life circumstances?
- Do you anticipate that He's going to communicate something intimate and applicable that you need to know to live this life with Him and for Him when you open your Bible? If you come to God with an open heart, He most certainly will.

Opening your heart before you open your Bible is how you set the table for the feast. Since God Himself prepared the meal, all you need to do is prepare your hungry heart.

My hope in this devotion is to inspire you to develop a pre-Bible-reading routine, one that helps you ready your heart for an encounter with God. Before you open His Word, gauge how open you are to His Word. Ask yourself, "Did I come to hear from the Lord today?" Or you can start with a simple prayer asking God to fulfill His many promises found in the Scriptures as you prepare to dive into them.

Lord, tell me great and hidden things that I have not known (Jer. 33:3). Open my eyes to spiritual truth so that I may behold wonderful things from Your law (Ps. 119:18). You made my ears to hear, my eyes to see, my mind to comprehend, and my heart to understand (Prov. 20:12; Deut. 29:4), so give me the ability to hear You and see You now, and open my mind and heart to understand the Scriptures (Luke 24:45). I ask all this in the name of Jesus, the clearest and kindest communicator, Amen.

Those verses have shaped my own pre-reading prayers. I'm drawn to the idea that God gives us the ability to know Him, the eyes to see Him, the ears to intimately hear His voice, and the mind to comprehend how His love enables us to live. Praying these Bible verses increases my hunger for the feast before I even dig in.

Since we are likening these forty days to a hearty meal, let's take a lesson from the family table. Before we feast on literal food, we pray and give thanks. Each and every time. How might our Bible reading change if we prayed before we feasted on His Word? Author and pastor Matt Smethhurst wrote, "I am convinced that a prayerless approach to God's Word is a major reason for the low-level dissatisfaction that hums beneath the surface of our lives."[1]

"Did I come to hear from the Lord today?"

What a powerful thought. It makes me wonder if the opposite might be true as well. Could a prayerful approach to God's Word be the key to a high level of satisfaction in our Christian lives? I think so.

I hope you're catching a vision of what it might look like to ready your heart for your time in the Word. First you are to open your heart, then you are to open your Bible. This is what it means to set the table for your feast.

I love that Pastor Keating encouraged us to get our hearts ready to receive the Word before His Sunday sermons, but this is a question we should be asking ourselves daily.

You don't need a pastor or a Bible teacher to lead you into the Word each day. Even though I'm here helping you apply God's Word to your life, you don't need me either. The Bible, dear friend, is a holy communication written by God to you, and accessing it doesn't require the preaching of a pastor or a bite-size devotion written by an author such as myself. Our commentary is intended to lead you deeper into His Word; however, we are not gatekeepers to the Word. Though we love to set the table for others to gather around, the reality is that you can pull up a chair anytime, day or night, to taste and see God's words for yourself.

Let the teaching of others on Sunday mornings whet your appetite for more of what God has served up for you in the pages of your Bible. The main course is an encounter with God Himself, through His written Word. Ask the Holy Spirit to open your eyes and ears, your heart and mind, then dig in.

Are you ready to hear from the Lord today? This is the place in our forty-day feast where you go from being a secondhand recipient of God's Word to a direct hearer. When we were children, our parents and teachers read us stories, fables, and fairy tales. As we grew up, however, we took those books from their loving hands and began reading the words for ourselves. That's what we're doing now. We're picking up our Bibles and reading them for ourselves. But this is no fairy tale.

There's a short verse in Job that applies to us today. Job said, "I had heard of you by the hearing of the ear, but now my eye sees you" (42:5 ESV).

Dear friend, you've heard God's Word spoken aloud. You've received teaching from His Word from pastors and Bible teachers—perhaps parents and grandparents too. Today is the day to take the Bible from their gracious hands and open it up for yourself. There's a bona fide feast set before you! Simply ask yourself this pre-reading question: "Did I come to hear from the Lord today?"

Lord, tell me great and hidden things that I have not known (Jer. 33:3). Open my eyes to spiritual truth so that I might behold wonderful things from Your law (Ps. 119:18). You made my ears to hear, my eyes to see, my mind to comprehend, and my heart to understand (Prov. 20:12; Deut. 29:4), so give me the ability to hear You and see You now, and open my mind and heart to understand the Scriptures (Luke 24:45). Teach me, for Your Word is life (Deut. 32:47)! I ask all this in the name of Jesus, the clearest and kindest communicator, Amen.

THE FEAST

Deuteronomy 32:1–47

FOOD FOR THOUGHT

The goal of these daily devotions is to whet your appetite for God's Word. My words are not the feast, merely an appetizer.

Deuteronomy 32 is a meaty portion, so I hope you made it to verse 47. What a powerful thought: His words are life! Highlight, asterisk, underline. Write it in the margin of your Bible or in this book if you prefer: "God, Your words are my very life!" Then write it in your heart!

day 17

LEARNING TO FEAST

For it is by grace you have been saved, through faith—and this is
not from yourselves, it is the gift of God—not by works, so that
no one can boast.

Ephesians 2:8–9

I LOVE A GOOD ACROSTIC. Especially one that sticks in my
brain and stays there for good. The first one I learned was this
definition of grace:

God's
Riches
At
Christ's
Expense

Even as a child I was able to understand it. God offered me
forgiveness from my sins because Jesus paid the price. G.R.A.C.E.
made that deep theological truth simple somehow. Yes, at a young

age, I believed it, accepted it, and received it. However, because I wasn't yet in touch with the reality of my own sin nature, God's grace felt more like a gentle hug than an extravagant gift. Years later, I'm sad to say, I finally came face-to-face with my need for such a gift. While I wish I could go back and undo some of the things I did, the reality is that my big sins finally allowed me to comprehend God's big grace.

I was lost and He found me.

I was a sinner and He saved me.

I was too poor to pay my debt, so He paid top dollar and wiped the ledger clean.

The Son of God became the riches of God to buy me back as a child of God.

Because He paid such a high price for my redemption, I now belong to Him! God's Riches At Christ's Expense. Once I grasped the reality of my costly salvation, I was desperate to dive in to the Word to better know my Savior. That desperation felt a lot like hunger. Perhaps that is why I started to feast.

While the G.R.A.C.E. acrostic creates a definitive sentence, other acrostics work like a step-by-step guide. Asheritah Ciuciu encourages her Bible-hungry friends to use this F.E.A.S.T. method: Focus on God, Engage the text, Assess the main idea, Spark transformation, and Turn to God in worship.[1] For the purpose of this chapter, however, I want to consider these main points to help us ingest and digest God's Word.

Fellowship

Eat

Apply

Savor

Trust

Fellowship. Given the lavish grace of God that brought you into a sincere friendship with Him through Christ, begin your time in His Word by simply fellowshiping with Him. Sit with Him as you would sit with a friend, for that is what He is. Begin with prayer; simply talk with the Triune God. Because of His grace, you get full access to God the Father, the Son, and the Holy Spirit. The feast always starts with friendship!

Eat. To eat God's Word must include both ingesting it and digesting it. We do that by first reading the text and then allowing it to settle into our hearts and minds so it can transform the way we live. If all we do is open it up and gobble it up, it will never get down into our figurative bellies and transform our literal lives.

Apply. When Matt and I were newlyweds, we sat under the teaching of Chuck Swindoll on Sunday mornings. After his sermon and final benediction, the congregation would immediately stand up and leave the sanctuary as the organist played a parting hymn. We often struggled to budge. Sitting in our seats as the sanctuary emptied, my husband and I would ask this question: If all that's true, how should we live?

Another word we could use for the A in this acrostic is *Act*. If God's Word is true, how should we act? How should we apply it to our lives? How should we live? God tells us clearly, "Do not merely listen to the word, and so deceive yourselves. Do what it says" (James 1:22). Don't leave the "pew" until you know what to do.

Savor. Just as a good meal shouldn't be gulped down quickly, reading God's Word is best when it's savored. That doesn't mean you always need great gobs of time to sit and study. However, taking your time at least a few days a week will help you eat until you are good and full! But this idea of savoring also goes with you as you move throughout your day. Scribble one of the verses you ingested on a notecard and tuck it in your pocket or leave it beside your coffee maker. Each time you return for another cup of courage to get you through your day, you'll be reminded to savor the only thing that truly can make you brave for the day ahead.

Trust. Just as applying and savoring God's Word aren't confined to the moments we read our Bibles, trusting God is an ongoing process as we live out His commands on a daily basis. Living a feasting life always requires trusting God and obeying Him—all day, every day.

Remember the story from day 11 about the J. H. Sammis hymn, "When We Walk with the Lord"? During the many months I spent writing this book, I often found myself singing those lyrics. Though I've already quoted them, I want you to read them (and maybe sing them) again:

> When we walk with the Lord
> in the light of His Word,
> what a glory He sheds *on our way!*
> While we do His good will,
> He abides with us still,
> and with all who will trust and obey.[2]

"On our way" is a powerful phrase! It's commonplace to think that our time with the Lord is confined to the moments we are actively reading at a table or praying down on our knees. But when we walk with God in the lamplight of His Word, He continually sheds His glorious light *on our way*. He goes with us. That's why, when we finish our Bible reading, we aren't actually finished. The feast is portable! We take it with us. We fill out pockets and our hearts with leftovers to last us all day long.

When we close our Bibles, we must not close our hearts to what we've learned.

My feasting friend, it's time to tie our two acrostics together: **Because of the G.R.A.C.E. of God, we F.E.A.S.T. on the Word of God.** He saved us for Himself, so we dive into His Word to know Him and learn to live for Him. We *fellowship* with the One who redeemed us, *eat* His Words and *apply* them to our lives, *savor* them as we ingest them and continue to savor them throughout the day, then we choose to actively *trust* God as we seek to obediently live out His decrees. When we close our Bibles, we must not close our hearts to what we've learned. Our Bible study continues as we apply the feast to our lives every moment of every day.

Because I don't want anything to hold you back from the feasting life, here's one more F.E.A.S.T. acrostic to inspire you:

Forget

Everything

And

Start

Today!

When it comes to feasting, nothing but the Bible can save, satisfy, sustain, or sanctify. Not another cup of coffee or another scroll through social media, not a leftover brownie, not a shopping cart full of stuff, not success at work or in your home. These temporary things cannot make you full—or help you become more like Christ. Only the grace of God can save you (Eph. 2:8–9). Only the love of God can satisfy you (Ps. 90:14). Only His ongoing presence can sustain you (Jer. 15:16–17). And only the Word of God can sanctify you (John 17:17). Forget everything else you've been shoving into your life and start *feasting* on Him!

Lord, thank You for Your generous love and Your sustaining grace. I accept the free gift of salvation because Jesus paid my debt. Because You bought me, I'm Yours now. Help me understand how to fellowship with You in Your Word. I want to eat it up, apply it to my life, savor it throughout my days, and trust and obey You. All day, every day. In the satisfying name of Jesus, Amen.

THE FEAST

Romans 3

FOOD FOR THOUGHT

As you feast on Romans 3, use my F.E.A.S.T. acrostic as a guide. Start by fellowshiping with the One who is the Word. He is your friend. Spend time talking with Him. Then, as you ingest His Word, ask Him to help you digest it and apply it to your life. Savor it as you go, then continue to trust and obey Him as you live it out.

day 18

HEY, Y'ALL

They were continually and faithfully devoting themselves to the instruction of the apostles, and to fellowship, to eating meals together and to prayers.

Acts 2:42 AMP

ALTHOUGH I WAS RAISED in Southern California, I always felt like I belonged just a little farther south. Texas captured my imagination in my teen years as I listened to country music and adopted "y'all" into my vocabulary. A few years after I graduated from college, I met and married a Texan, then moved to Dallas to be his bride.

During the first year of our marriage, Matt and I joined a Sunday school class for young couples. On Sunday mornings after the main service, we gathered in a small room down the hall from the sanctuary. Taking turns bringing bagels and donuts, we spent that hour "breaking bread," both literally and figuratively. Balancing little plastic plates full of pastries on our knees, we made room for our Bibles there too. Crumbs fell on open pages, and it all tasted good.

Feasting in Christian fellowship is twofold and doubly satisfying, for we don't just fill our bellies, we satiate our hearts and minds with biblical truth that satisfies and transforms us. God's Word, studied in community, shapes our lives to look more like Christ both corporately and individually.

In that Sunday school class, we worked our way through entire books of the Bible, applying what we read to how we lived. Sometimes guest speakers would teach from the Bible on topics that were relevant to us as newlyweds. But always, regardless of the style of Bible study, we feasted on the Holy Scriptures and regularly broke bread together.

I love the Amplified Bible's translation of today's opening Scripture because it emphasizes the early church's ongoing devotion to one another and to the Lord: "They were *continually and faithfully* devoting themselves to the instruction of the apostles, and to fellowship, to eating meals together, and to prayers" (Acts 2:42, emphasis added).

Sunday mornings at church, midweek Bible studies, and eventually at other times as well, Matt and I learned to feast with friends. Not long after we began attending that class, one of the couples invited us over for dinner. Kelli and Lee lived in a little apartment not far from the church. As our husbands grilled chicken on the tiny hibachi grill our hosts had received as a wedding gift, Kelli and I chitchatted in the kitchen while we warmed crusty French bread in the oven and tossed a salad. I'm sure there were some deeply spiritual conversations shared around the bistro-size table that night, but what I remember most was the laughter—and Girard's Champagne Vinaigrette. I loved the salad Kelli served so much that I purchased a bottle of her favorite dressing the very next week. What a picture of Christian fellowship! We learn from one another and ultimately change some of our habits as a direct result.

By the time Matt and I celebrated our one-year anniversary, we were deeply rooted in a thriving community of Bible-believing friends. In addition to attending the Sunday school class and Tuesday morning Bible study, Kelli and I hosted baby showers for some of the ladies in our group, and our husbands attended an evening Bible study taught by one of the older men in the church.

Though I grew up attending Sunday school classes as a child and even led Bible studies throughout my college and postcollege years, I had never experienced Christian community quite like this before. Perhaps it's because I had moved into a region where they didn't just say "y'all," they lived it too.

There are so many rich Bible passages that focus on the importance of community—a veritable feast of verses—but the passage below, in its entirety, has helped me understand the importance of Christian fellowship.

> Therefore, *brothers and sisters*, since *we* have confidence to enter the Most Holy Place by the blood of Jesus, by a new and living way opened for *us* through the curtain, that is, his body, and since *we* have a great priest over the house of God, let *us* draw near to God with a sincere heart and with the full assurance that faith brings, having *our* hearts sprinkled to cleanse *us* from a guilty conscience and having *our* bodies washed with pure water. Let *us* hold unswervingly to the hope *we* profess, for he who promised is faithful. And let *us* consider how *we* may spur *one another* on toward love and good deeds, not giving up meeting *together*, as some are in the habit of doing, but encouraging *one another*—and all the more as you see the Day approaching. (Heb. 10:19–25, emphasis added)

I encourage you to read this passage again. Slowly this time. As you do, pay particular attention to all the italicized plural pronouns and inclusive references to community. I'm afraid that the tendency of most people today (within our churches and beyond them) is to remain private and guarded, to quietly deal with sin-struggles. Each man and woman trying to understand and apply God's Word to their own lives. However, these verses cry out, "Community!" It is my hope that each emphasized word emboldens your heart to reach out and invite people into the journey with you—and into your home as you break bread together.

Today's Christian culture reminds me a bit of our first house in Texas. I loved every nook and cranny of our little home on

Brunchberry Lane except for one thing—our garage opened into the back alley. We drove down the alley and closed the garage door before walking into our house. When it was time to go somewhere again, we left the same way. As a result, we rarely ran into our neighbors.

Some people attend church this way. They arrive right on time or a few minutes late and then sneak out quickly, never joining life groups or attending Bible studies. They miss out on both the literal meals and so many rich Bible meals too.

Let's purpose to not live that way as Christians. The final charge in the Hebrews passage concludes: "And let us *consider* how we may *spur* one another on toward love and good deeds, *not giving up meeting together*, as some are in the habit of doing, but *encouraging one another*—and all the more as you see the Day approaching" (10:24–25, emphasis added). What a muscular, intentional charge! There are so many active verbs calling us to open wide our front doors and engage in fellowship with other believers.

We were made for fellowship—with God and with one another. For more than two thousand years, Jewish men and boys have gathered to study the earliest Scriptures. To the early, fledgling churches, Paul sent letters and had them read aloud; then the letters were passed to other congregations. Only since the fifteenth-century invention of the printing press and the expansion of literacy over the last two centuries have people been able to routinely hold God's Word in their own two hands and read it behind their own closed doors. Let's not allow the fact that we can read our Bibles for ourselves keep us by ourselves!

> *Let's not allow the fact that we can read our Bibles for ourselves keep us by ourselves!*

You should absolutely read your Bible on your own; just don't let it keep you alone. You were made for community, and so was the Word of God. As you look for ways to dive into your Bible, actively pursue opportunities to study it with others. Read it together, share what you're learning, take turns hosting one another in your homes, and break bread as you feast on the Bread of Life together.

And when you are tempted to give up "as some are in the habit of doing," be encouraged by the example of the early church: "They were *continually and faithfully* devoting themselves to the instruction of the apostles, and to fellowship, to eating meals together and to prayers" (Acts 2:42 AMP, emphasis added). Then chase those words down with this sweet morsel: "But encourage one another daily, as long as it is called 'Today,' so that none of you may be hardened by sin's deceitfulness" (Heb. 3:13).

Y'all, if we were actually studying God's Word together today, I'd reach over and take your hand before bowing my head to pray.

Oh, Lord! Thank You for Your church. Thank You for giving us a place to study Your Word, lift our voices in praise, break bread together, encourage one another in godliness, and warn one another against sinfulness. Give me the courage to say yes to opening my front door as an extension of Your church, inviting brothers and sisters to gather in my home over Your Word. In Jesus's all-inclusive name, Amen.

THE FEAST

Acts 2
(Don't forget to search for the
inclusive language in verses 42–47!)

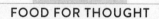

FOOD FOR THOUGHT

Here is your dessert after the feast: reach out and invite someone to break bread with you very soon.

day 19

GOD-BREATHED

All Scripture is God-breathed and is useful for teaching, rebuking, correcting and training in righteousness, so that the servant of God may be thoroughly equipped for every good work.

2 Timothy 3:16–17

YESTERDAY WE CONSIDERED the importance of community when reading the Bible. Today we're going to build upon that foundation of fellowship as we consider inviting the person of the Holy Spirit to be our dining companion. In fact, we need to invite the Holy Spirit before we invite any other person to join us. Let's pull up a chair at the table of this feast and eagerly anticipate how the presence of the Holy Spirit might enliven our time in the Holy Scriptures.

More than your favorite Bible teacher, your closest friend, or the influencers you follow online, the Holy Spirit of God can help you understand the holy Word of God better than anyone else. After all, the Holy Spirit is the author! That's right. All sixty-six individual books in your Bible—written over the course of 1,600 years and

penned by over forty authors who wrote in multiple languages—
were actually authored by the Holy Spirit. It was He who breathed
those precious promises onto parchment
for the edification of God's people.

The apostle Peter tells us, "No prophecy
in Scripture ever came from the prophet's
own understanding, or from human initia-
tive. No, those prophets were moved by
the Holy Spirit, and they spoke from God"
(2 Pet. 1:20–21 NLT). And the prophet
Samuel tells us, "The Spirit of the LORD
spoke through me; his word was on my
tongue" (2 Sam. 23:2).

*The same Holy
Spirit who inspired
the writing of
the Bible inspires
us in the reading
of the Bible.*

The same Holy Spirit who inspired the
writing of the Bible inspires us in the reading of the Bible. Therefore, all that is necessary for a person to read, understand, and
apply God's Word are these three things: the inspired Word, the
Holy Spirit who inspired it, and a human heart that is eager to be
inspired. In his book *Foundations of the Christian Faith*, theologian
James Montgomery Boice wrote:

> The Bible is something more than a body of revealed truths, a col-
> lection of books verbally inspired by God. It is also the living voice
> of God. The living God speaks through its pages. Therefore, it is not
> to be valued as a sacred object to be placed on a shelf and neglected,
> but as holy ground, where people's hearts and minds may come
> into vital contact with the living, gracious, and disturbing God. For
> a proper perspective on Scripture and for a valid understanding of
> revelation, there must be constant interworking of these factors; an
> infallible and authoritative Word, the activity of the Holy Spirit in
> interpreting and applying that Word, and a receptive human heart.
> No true knowledge of God takes place without these elements.[1]

Take a moment to consider in your heart these questions:

- Do I believe that the Bible is the authoritative and abso-
  lute, inerrant, and infallible Word of God?

- Do I recognize the role the Holy Spirit played in the writing of the Bible?
- Am I willing to invite the Holy Spirit to the feast?
- Do I have a receptive and teachable heart?

If the answer to all of these questions is yes, then the next logical step is to embrace the truth of the apostle Paul's words to Timothy: "All Scripture is God-breathed and is useful for teaching, rebuking, correcting and training in righteousness, so that the servant of God may be thoroughly equipped for every good work" (2 Tim. 3:16–17).

The New International Version translation uses the hyphenated phrase "God-breathed" when many other translations render it as "inspired by God." Both are correct, but many scholars agree that the original Greek word *theopneustos* most accurately translates as "God-breathed."[2] One fluid breath and one fluid phrase. And since we are taking a moment to consider the original language and text, it's exciting to discover that the Hebrew word for "spirit," as in the Holy Spirit, is *ruakh*, which translates into both "breath" and "wind."[3] In essence, the Spirit of God is God's breath.

The Holy Spirit breathed out the Word into the world. His exhale may have come through the mouths and quills of men, but it was always the Holy Spirit who inspired and enabled—which means that He can inspire and enable us to understand and apply each God-breathed word! We believe that all Scripture is "useful for teaching, rebuking, correcting and training in righteousness," but we need the Spirit's ongoing help being taught, rebuked, corrected, and trained. Yes, even rebuked and corrected by Scripture, so that we might know what needs to change in our lives.

This is why we must invite the Holy Spirit to the feast we're so eager to enjoy. It is the Holy Spirit who is able to teach and train us, convict and correct us. As we open up our Bibles and open up our hearts, the Holy Spirit breathes His Word into our very lives and helps us to see with spiritual eyes what it all means and how we are to live in response.

However, just as it is with any gracious guest, the Holy Spirit is awaiting an invitation to the table. Though He's the One who breathed the feast into existence, He is waiting for us to set a place for Him and exhale a humble, "Teach me." I'm reminded of the invitation in Brian and Katie Torwalt's song, "Holy Spirit": "Holy Spirit, you are welcome here."[4]

We've already considered how we might prepare our hearts for the feast by asking, "Did I truly come to hear from the Lord today?" Now we're pushing our hearts to do just that—to hear from Him, the Holy Spirit Himself. **The Bible is the only book in which the reader has direct and constant access to the author.** While you may be able to find me on social media and send me a message, the Author of your Bible is available to you 24/7, anytime, anywhere.

Holy Spirit, thank You for breathing the Bible into the hearts of simple servants. Will You breathe it into my heart too? Use these verses to teach me and train me in righteousness, as You rebuke me and reshape me into a more beautiful display of You-in-me. I've come to hear from You today. Holy Spirit, breathe. Amen.

THE FEAST

2 Timothy 3

FOOD FOR THOUGHT

Once you've enjoyed 2 Timothy 3 as your first course, go back for seconds! On your next pass through, invite the Holy Spirit to not only teach and train you, but also to rebuke and correct you. It is possible to have a form of godliness that looks nothing like God. We don't want that, and God certainly doesn't want that for us. Invite the Holy Spirit to breathe 2 Timothy 3 into your life today.

day 20

WHERE TO BEGIN

In the beginning God . . .

Genesis 1:1

TODAY'S SCRIPTURE is a partial phrase but a complete promise. Half a verse but a whole truth. Before God created one single thing, He simply existed. The first four words in the Bible form an incomplete sentence but paint a complete picture of who God always has been and always will be—eternal.

In the beginning God . . .

Here and now, God . . .

Tomorrow, God . . .

Forevermore, God . . .

Before you consider where to begin your Bible reading, consider the lack of God's beginning. Start there. Before you try to figure out a reading plan, meditate on the vastness of the One who planned forever. Let the enormity of His presence, from eternity past to eternity future, overwhelm you more than the thought of reading your Bible does. Yes, start with this half verse first: "In the beginning God . . ." Instead of worrying about the scope of your undertaking, revel in His eternal undertaking. No beginning, no end. **While His holy book is big, His holy bigness can't be contained in any one Bible reading plan, so let that go for a moment.**

"In the beginning God . . ."

Regardless of which book of the Bible you read first, God . . .

Whatever time of day you read, God . . .

Wherever you sit, God . . .

Whatever questions you ask, God . . .

Don't get me wrong, I'm a planner. Sometimes I follow a plan that helps me read through the entire Bible in a year. But there are also times when I can't keep up the pace or I'm inspired to camp out in one verse, one chapter, or one book. In later devotions, I'll talk more about both reading the Bible through over the course of a year and spending extended time in just one sliver of it. However, let's not race off into a Bible reading plan before we acknowledge God's plan, regardless of where we start, how many chapters we read, or what Bible study method we follow.

God's plan, each time we crack open our Bible, is to bring together the only three eternal things in existence: Himself, His Word, and His people. That's right, the Bible is eternal, God is eternal, *and so is your soul.* While each person gets to choose where they will abide forever—heaven in His presence or hell without Him—each human soul lives on eternally in one destination or the other. Therefore, when we meet with our eternal God in His eternal Word, it holds eternal significance regardless of where we open it up.

Temporal moments with God hold eternal significance.

When this eternal trifecta comes together (God, His Word, and you) the result is always the same: God accomplishes what He intends to accomplish. When we are with Him in His Word, His Word gets planted as an eternal seed in us. If the soil of our hearts is receptive, that seed will grow to achieve the purpose for which God planted it. Always. Every single time. No matter how long a passage, how short a verse, or how much time we linger over the lesson—temporal moments with God hold eternal significance. They will never be void, empty, or wasted. Here's how we know this is true:

> As the rain and the snow
>   come down from heaven,
> and do not return to it
>   without watering the earth
> and making it bud and flourish,
>   so that it yields seed for the sower and bread for
>   the eater,
> so is my word that goes out from my mouth:
>   It will not return to me empty,
> but will accomplish what I desire
>   and achieve the purpose for which I sent it.
>   (Isa. 5:10–11)

In the beginning, God eternal created not only the heavens and the earth, but He also purposed your life. Before the universe was spoken into existence, thoughts of you existed. Though the things of earth will one day pass away forever, you won't. You will live forever once this present life is over. The specifics of your eternal address depend upon your acceptance or rejection of God's Son and His free gift of salvation. But either way your soul will live on. Accepting Jesus as your eternal soul's Savior is the way into His eternal kingdom, but rejecting Him will usher you into a forever separation from Him, in hell. This is why our time in God's eternal Word is so important. It prepares us to enjoy Him both now and forevermore.

And so, today, instead of focusing on *which* seeds need to get planted first, I invite you to focus on how receptive your heart is. The soil of your heart must be soft and supple before the Master Gardener scatters seeds in the field.

Jesus shared a parable about this very thing:

A farmer went out to sow his seed. As he was scattering the seed, some fell along the path, and the birds came and ate it up. Some fell on rocky places, where it did not have much soil. It sprang up quickly, because the soil was shallow. But when the sun came up, the plants were scorched, and they withered because they had no root. Other seed fell among thorns, which grew up and choked the plants. Still other seed fell on good soil, where it produced a crop—a hundred, sixty or thirty times what was sown. Whoever has ears, let them hear. (Matt. 13:3–9)

In a previous devotion, I encouraged you to ask the question, "Did I come to hear from the Lord today?" Today we aren't just nodding our heads, we're rolling up our sleeves and tilling the soil. It's time to get on our knees and get our hands in the dirt as we ask some follow-up questions:

- Am I willing to do what God instructs?
- Am I willing to cultivate the field of my faith life once the seeds are planted?
- Will I lay myself out in the Sonlight and plant myself beside streams of living water?
- Am I committed to seeing the fruit of His Spirit growing on the laurels of my life?
- Am I eager to see a crop of God's righteousness spring up from within me—even if it means giving up some of the rotten fruit I've long loved?
- Am I willing to allow the Master Gardener access into my private garden plot, day after day, to prune what needs cutting back so that I might bear more fruit?
- Will I allow His Word to point out the weeds and the rocks I need to pull out and throw out—and the behaviors and thoughts I need to uproot?

The prophet Isaiah spoke of God's people as "oaks of righteousness, a planting of the LORD for the display of his splendor" (61:3). God will accomplish what He set out to accomplish in us and through us. But we get to actively join Him in the process. Let's ready the soil of our hearts for the seeds He is willing to plant in the garden of our lives, that we might become "a display of His splendor" both now and forevermore!

I love how The Message captures this theme: "In simple humility, let our gardener, God, landscape you with the Word, making a salvation-garden of your life" (James 1:21).

It doesn't matter where you start reading. **If you are eager to receive eternal truth from our eternal God through His eternal Word, your life will be eternally changed as a result.** It's a promise. Just as the rain and the snow come down and water the earth, His Word will nourish your eternal soul and accomplish what He intends!

Dear Lord, thank You for all the seeds You have planted and all the ones You'll tuck into the soft soil of my life in the future. Help me to receive them so that I become a beautiful and eternal display of Your splendor, both now and forevermore. Landscape me with Your Word, so that I might become a salvation garden! In the forever name of Jesus, Amen.

THE FEAST

Matthew 13:1–43
John 15:1–8

FOOD FOR THOUGHT

Spend some time pondering the truth that you are an eternal being. Just as God and His Word will live forever, so will you. But you get to choose where you'll spend your forever life—with Him or without Him. Allow His forever Word to show you how to abide in His forever presence.

day 21

INQUISITIVE

Ask, and it will be given to you; seek, and you will find; knock, and it will be opened to you.

Matthew 7:7 ESV

DURING THE FIRST HALF of our feast, I attempted to woo you to God's Word by celebrating how good and sweet it is. However, if you are ever going to taste and see His loving-goodness for yourself, you'll need to do more than simply read it; you'll need to dig in and study. **It is possible to read God's Word and not taste it or allow its sweetness to permeate your life, but it is *not possible* to come to God's Word with a sincere hunger and miss out on the flavor of His goodness.**

Today we will consider how to not only read God's Word but also how to study it and apply it to our lives by asking three simple questions. My personal method of Bible study can be summed up in one word: *inquisitive.* When I come to the Lord in a passage of Scripture, I come to Him with questions. Of course, I'm not the first person to do this. Before I share with you my simplified inquisitive method of Bible study, let me introduce you to its predecessor: inductive Bible study.

Inductive Bible study is a common method of studying God's Word. It offers an easy-to-follow, three-step approach. Whether you are coming to the text with no Bible knowledge at all or a wealth of wisdom cultivated over years of reading God's Word, the inductive method of Bible study can help you dig deep into the Scriptures, then apply them to your life in a fresh way.

This style of Bible study began with Howard Tillman Kuist and Wilbert W. White at the Bible Seminary in New York. In 1899 White wrote the first inductive Bible study curriculum for the YMCA. Later, Howard Kuist and Charles Haley honed the method further when they taught at Princeton Theological Seminary. By the 1940s and 1950s, inductive studies of the Bible were being created by InterVarsity Christian Fellowship, the Navigators, and Youth with a Mission.[1]

More recently, Kay Arthur's Precept ministry has carried the inductive Bible study method into our generation of Bible readers. In her book *How to Study Your Bible*, Kay wrote, "Inductive Bible study draws you into personal interaction with the Scripture and thus with the God of the Scriptures so that your beliefs are based on a prayerful understanding and legitimate interpretation of Scripture—truth that transforms you when you live by it."[2]

Here are the three steps of inductive Bible study, often referred to by their acronym, O.I.A.:

Observation

Interpretation

Application

Observation: What does it say? Begin by reading through the text multiple times, slowly and carefully, asking clarifying questions as you go: "What does the text say? Where does this take place? Who is this about? Why might the cultural and historical context matter?" Use the five Ws—who, what, when, where, why—and how.

Circling repeated words, possible themes, and patterns of cause and effect can all lead to further understanding. Some people use multicolored highlighters to draw attention to the main characters, locations, and the main action words. Give yourself at least five to seven minutes to dig into the text through observation. You may be able to read quickly, but it's not possible to study quickly. So take your time.

Interpretation: What does it mean? Once you have made some observations, it's time to form some conclusions. Summarize the main theme of your text, then consider why it is significant. Take your time to interpret what you have observed. For example, you might interpret truths about the nature or character of God on display in that passage. Don't rush. Allow at least five minutes for this step. It's important to know what God is telling you about Himself before you apply it to yourself.

Application: What does it mean for my life? This is where it gets personal and transformational. The application portion of Bible study is often the step most people race past, but it is the most important part of all if you want God's Word to leave a mark on your life. To consider application, ask questions like these: "Is there something I need to do (or stop doing) in response to what God has revealed through His Word? Is there a promise I need to believe, a warning I need to heed, or a command I need to obey?"

As you practice these steps, you'll grow to understand the big picture of God's story, as well as the intimate, individual scenes that communicate God's heart one short passage at a time. You'll become more comfortable making observations, interpreting the text, and applying it to your life in a way that leads not only to head knowledge but also to heart change. The inductive approach to Bible study helps us get to the heart of what we are reading so God can get to our hearts—and change our hearts and minds and, ultimately, our beliefs and behaviors.

I've mentioned before that most Bible-believing Christians (and non-Christians too) don't read the Bible because they don't understand it. For that very reason, the inductive method of Bible study is perfect! It begins with questions, assumes that we do not understand what's being said, and allows us to arrive at biblical conclusions on our own—with the help of the Holy Spirit, of course.

It's okay to have questions. When we are inquisitive, God is communicative. We can bring all of our clarifying questions to the One whose Spirit loves to clarify and help us apply all that we learn to our life each day.

Author Tara-Leigh Cobble offers this encouragement: "The questions we ask of the Bible impact the wisdom we glean from it."[3] If you are eager to glean wisdom that applies directly to your life, come to the Bible curious, with questions, and eager for answers.

> *When we are inquisitive, God is communicative.*

Practice making observations and forming thoughtful interpretations, and then allow the Spirit to help you arrive at transformative applications.

Which reminds me, don't forget to bookend your time in the Bible with prayer. Start and end your reading by thanking God for His Word, then ask Him to not only give you the eyes to see, the ears to hear, and the mind to understand, but also a willingness to respond. **If we are inquisitive and God is communicative, then we ought to get to the place where we are demonstrative because His Word is transformative.**

Whether I am studying on my own, with a group of close friends, leading an online Bible study for many, or teaching my kids around the kitchen table, I often use a simplified version of the inductive method. After digging in to the text to best understand the biblical context, these are the questions that help me apply it to my life:

- What did I learn about God?
- What did I learn about myself?
- How do I need to live differently as a result?

Moving forward, I will sometimes include these three questions in the "Food for Thought" section at the end of the devotion. Let's be people who don't merely read our Bibles but study them too so that we might taste and see how good the God of the Bible truly is!

Lord, I want to learn how to learn. I'm willing to try new Bible study methods to know You better and apply Your transforming Word to my life. I confess that I need some transformation. Holy Spirit, guide me to the questions and the answers, then give me the courage to live differently as a result. I pray all this in the name of Jesus, the One who is the answer to every question. Amen.

THE FEAST

Matthew 7

FOOD FOR THOUGHT

During today's Bible reading, ask yourself:

- What did I learn about God?
- What did I learn about myself?
- How do I need to live differently as a result?

As we consider various methods of Bible study, remember that no formula can save us—that's Jesus's job. Multicolored highlighters can highlight truth, but only Jesus is the Truth. Questions help us find our answer, but only Jesus is the Answer.

Bible studies don't save. Jesus saves. Studying your Bible simply allows you to know the One who is our Savior.

day 22

READING THE BIBLE
IN CONTEXT

The temple, the LORD's temple, was filled with a cloud. And because of the cloud, the priests were not able to continue ministering, for the glory of the LORD filled God's temple.

2 Chronicles 5:13–14 CSB

ONE EARLY MORNING, I came out of my bedroom before the sun was in the sky and found my thirteen-year-old in a chair beside a lamp, reading his Bible. "Mom, listen to this!" he said as he turned back a page.

On the day the tabernacle, the tent of the covenant law, was set up, the cloud covered it. From evening till morning the cloud above the tabernacle looked like fire. That is how it continued to be; the cloud covered it, and at night it looked like fire. Whenever the cloud lifted from above the tent, the Israelites set out; wherever the cloud settled, the Israelites encamped. (Num. 9:15–17)

I sat down on the couch opposite him and marveled, "That's incredible, Asher. But what exactly is it about that passage that you like?"

He told me that it reminded him of the pillar of cloud that went before the people of Israel in the daytime and the pillar of fire that led them in the night (Exod. 13:21). "God wasn't just leading his people with those things," Asher explained, "I think He was actually in them too. Remember when God gave Moses the Ten Commandments? I read that God actually came down in the cloud" (Exod. 34:5).

That's when I jumped in and said, "And when God first spoke to Moses from within the burning bush, He was in the fire there as well" (Exod. 3).

Asher took out his pen and began writing in the margin of his Bible, so I quietly walked into the kitchen and made him a sugar-free decaf iced latte. Not all our encounters are this sweet, especially early in the morning, but I had to celebrate that this one was extra special.

Later in the day, I remembered another Bible story I had read a month or two earlier. At the time, I was about as weary as I had ever been. I was worn-out from leading Bible studies and worn-out from mothering and worn-out from all the tasks, big and small, that God had called me to. And I confess I wanted to quit.

When I came across 2 Chronicles 5:13–14, I knew the Lord was speaking to me in a very personal way, so I read it again and again, day after day, for over a week. Here's what I read and reread: "The temple, the Lord's temple, was filled with a cloud. And because of the cloud, the priests were not able to continue ministering, for the glory of the Lord filled God's temple" (CSB).

Using the inductive Bible study method we discussed yesterday, I was able to understand the passage in context. The story takes place right after King Solomon built God's house, the temple in Jerusalem. While Moses oversaw the construction of the mobile tent-tabernacle in the wilderness, it was Solomon who had the joy of building a permanent home for the Lord in the promised land, 480 years later. The king assigned different families from within the tribe of Levi to serve the Lord in different capacities within the temple.

Once the construction was complete, the Lord's Spirit came down in the form of a dense cloud and took up residency within His new house. But the cloud was so thick that the Levitical priests couldn't go in to do their work.

Sometimes as I read Bible stories, God lifts them up out of their historical context and applies them to the context of my life. How kind He is to speak to me so personally from the pages of this ancient book.

Though I'm not a Levitical priest, God has called me to do a job in my home and out in the world, as a mother and as a minister of the gospel. But sometimes I desperately want to stop "going to work." I don't want to do the job He has assigned me. As I read this passage, however, I was convicted that the Lord's presence was the only thing that stopped the priests from doing their tasks. The lesson was clear: Unless God crowds me out (with His glory), I have to keep showing up (for His glory)!

I share this story as a very real example of how we are to read the Bible in its context and then connect the dots, as Asher and I did together, while inviting the Holy Spirit to make it relevant to the context of our lives. When we earnestly apply ourselves to the study of God's Word, His Word begins to apply to our lives.

The Bible is about Him, not us.

The Bible is about Him, not us. It's a historical drama, not a modern-day tale. And yet, in His kindness, the Lord allows His living Word to transcend "His-story" and descend upon our stories today, like the cloud of His presence. Simply amazing. Scripture really is living, active, and applicable (Heb. 4:12). Over and over, day after day, generation after generation.

At the beginning of today's reading, I shared how Asher jotted notes in the margins beside Numbers 9. After he left for school, I peeked inside his Bible and read what he'd written: "The Lord was in the cloud over the tabernacle, and He was also in the pillar of cloud and the pillar of fire that led the Israelites through the desert.

THAT IS CRAZY!" Under his note, I wrote, "Son, I pray that you sense the Lord's leading throughout your life as well. Love, Mom." With the help of the Holy Spirit, I want my son to know the wisdom and knowledge that comes from reading his Bible in context, as well as the joy and discernment that is available when applied to the context of his life. And I pray the same for you.

Lord, You are the God of Abraham, Isaac, and Jacob. The people of Israel are Your people, and their ancient story reveals Your redemptive plan for each of us today. Help me understand the narrative of Your love throughout history, that I might experience Your love and Your purposes today. I ask this in the transcendent name of Jesus, Amen.

THE FEAST

Exodus 3

FOOD FOR THOUGHT

Which comes more naturally for you, reading Bible stories in their historical context or applying Bible stories to the context of your life? The feast of Exodus 3 is a wonderful passage with which we can practice both. Read it in the context of the biblical story, then ask yourself these questions:

- What did I learn about God?
- What did I learn about myself?
- How do I need to live differently as a result?

day 23

[INSERT YOUR NAME HERE]

For the word of God is alive and active. Sharper than any double-edged sword, it penetrates even to dividing soul and spirit, joints and marrow; it judges the thoughts and attitudes of the heart.

Hebrews 4:12

IN YESTERDAY'S DEVOTION I shared one of my favorite Bible study skills: reading the Bible in context and then applying it to the context of our lives. Today we are going to learn to insert our names into God's Word, believing that God is speaking directly to us.

A few years ago I published a parenting series on social media that I called "[Hey Mom]." Each short post started with a familiar Bible verse that included the bracketed words, "[Hey Mom]." Here's an example:

[Hey Mom] Let us not become weary in doing good, for at the proper time we will reap a harvest if we do not give up. (Gal. 6:9)[1]

From there I applied the verse to common parenting challenges. I wanted to encourage moms that God's ancient Word is alive and active and incredibly applicable to the work they do with their children each day. Though they may grow weary in doing the good work of mothering, they can press into this promise and press on, for at the proper time they will reap a harvest in their homes if they do not give up.

Here's another favorite [Hey Mom] verse:

[Hey Mom] Do not be overcome by evil, but overcome evil with good. (Rom. 12:21)

Every parent wants to do right when their children do wrong, but in stressful, triggered moments we often jump in and holler at the kids or simply blame and shame them. Of course, those tactics don't work. Lucky for us, God's Word penetrates each parenting problem and tells us that we can overcome our children's wrong actions with our right reactions—countering their evil with our good. As a matter of fact, God the Father shows us time and time again what gentle, patient parenting looks like—when we read our Bibles looking for it.[2]

My desire with the "[Hey Mom]" series was to show moms that God's Word is applicable right where they are. His Word was written to them and for them in that specific season of their lives. And that's true not just for moms and dads but for everyone, in each and every season. Men and women, young and old, God speaks to each of us personally as we open our hearts and open His Word. Today when I sit down to share a Bible verse on social media, I often include these bracketed words instead: "[Insert your name here]."

When I'm reading my Bible aloud with one of my children or studying it with a friend, I often insert their name for added emphasis. Likewise, when I read it quietly by myself, I invite God to speak my name into the yielded places of my own teachable heart.

Whether I'm reading long passages chock-full of instructions for godly living or a familiar Bible story, I'm always listening for God's voice to slip my name in and personalize His message to me.

While our Bibles are all about *Him*, He is all about us. So much so that He sent His Son, who is the Word, to chase us down and live out the message before our very eyes. Even today, all these years after Jesus walked the earth and the Spirit inspired the writing of the Bible, His words lift off the page and apply to our everyday lives.

Bible teacher Beth Moore wrote,

> The spectacular thing about Scripture . . . is that, like no other book held in human hands, its ink may be dry but it is the furthest thing from dead. The words are alive and active, and the Holy Spirit who inspired them can animate the most familiar passage and spring it to fresh life in your soul.[3]

That is exactly the promise Scripture makes about itself: "For the word of God is alive and active. Sharper than any double-edged sword, it penetrates even to dividing soul and spirit, joints and marrow; it judges the thoughts and attitudes of the heart" (Heb. 4:12).

While our Bibles are all about Him, *He is all about us.*

The Greek word translated "active" is *energēs*, from which we derive other words, such as "energy" and "energizing." God's Word is living and causes us to live; it is active and activates our hearts and minds to live right. This ancient scroll is not far off or irrelevant, but present and applicable. The Scriptures are not dead but alive, and they bring us to life. Even when our souls feel nearly dead, on the surgeon's table in need of life-saving measures, God's Word can revive our weary souls.

Speaking of soul surgery, the Greek word translated "sword" in this passage is *machaira*. This type of blade isn't commonly used in battle. Most soldiers would not carry one into war. Instead, this knife is a small and lightweight, double-edged blade that a surgeon would use. This small blade wasn't created to take life, but to save it. It was sharp and thin enough to penetrate flesh. In the hands of a skilled physician, it was capable of dividing joints and tendons, but in the loving hands of the Great Physician, it is able to separate the soul from the spirit, one's thoughts and attitude clean out of a soiled heart. Incredibly, a *machaira* is also the type of blade a fisherman might keep on his belt. Lucky for us, Jesus is both a fisher of people and a healer of people. And His Word is the tool He uses. **His Word cuts out what is sick in us, then points us to health, wholeness, and holiness.**

It is my greatest hope that you find Jesus as you open His Word each day. And as you encounter Him, on the figurative operating table beneath His double-edged sword, I pray you hear your name clearly spoken from each Bible page.

Today, before you open your Bible and feast on the main course of Scripture, let me first serve up dessert in the form of one of the sweetest passages in the whole Bible, a perfect promise to personalize:

> For God so loved [insert your name here] that he gave his one and only Son, that [if] [insert your name here] believes in him [she/he] shall not perish but have eternal life. For God did not send his Son into the world to condemn [insert your name here], but to save [insert your name here] through him. (John 3:16–17, author's paraphrase)

I hope God uses those sweet verses to remind you just how applicable and personal the whole Bible is.

Lord God, You speak so clearly. Thank You for using Your Word to cut deep down into my heart, separating my wrong thoughts, attitudes, and understanding from what is biblically true. I pray in the name of Jesus, the Great Physician, who is ready and waiting to perform surgery each time I open His Word, Amen.

THE FEAST

Colossians 3:1–17

FOOD FOR THOUGHT

As you ingested Colossians 3:1–17, did you notice all the wonderful places to slip your name into the passage? If not, I encourage you to read it again, out loud perhaps. Insert your name throughout, as though God is speaking directly to you. Because He is. Then ask yourself these powerful questions:

- What did I learn about God?
- What did I learn about myself?
- How do I need to live differently as a result?

day 24

GENESIS TO REVELATION

My son, be attentive to my words;
incline your ear to my sayings.
Let them not escape from your sight;
keep them within your heart.
For they are life to those who find them.

Proverbs 4:20–22 ESV

MY GRANDPA read through the Bible four times before he believed it. Though he attended church during his growing up years, he hadn't yet put his faith in Christ. Truth be told, the main reason he went to church at all was because, in his own words, "That's where the pretty girls were." Back in his early twenties, sometime around 1936, Grandpa purchased an old, early Ford Model T for twenty-some dollars. While it was already a broken-down, antiquated car by that time, he fixed it up so he could pick up the young women in the neighborhood and take them to church.

All was going according to plan until Grandpa asked the pastor's daughter out on a date. She asked him, then and there, if he had put his full faith in Jesus as his personal Lord and Savior. When Grandpa couldn't say that he had, she told him that she wouldn't date him, then held to her conviction as he read through the Bible, cover to cover, again and again and again. After his fourth time through, he believed. While my grandpa didn't end up marrying that pastor's daughter, she will always hold a special place in my heart.

We are now at the place in our forty-day feast where we are considering different ways to read our Bibles in an effort to know God intimately, to experience His love personally, and to allow His message of redemption to speak into our lives. Today, I encourage you to prayerfully consider reading it through from beginning to end, from Genesis to Revelation. If the whole Bible was given to us, can't we give ourselves the gift of reading the whole thing?

While there is no hocus-pocus magic that happens just because you crack the cover at the beginning and make it through to the end, there is a miracle available to those who are willing to seek God in such a committed way. Speaking on behalf of God, the prophet Jeremiah declared, "You will seek me and find me when you seek me with all your heart" (29:13). **Making the commitment to seek God in His whole Word will take your whole heart.** It will take time, energy, and prioritizing the seeking and the finding— but if you don't prioritize it, how will you find Him? Not for the sake of the pastor's daughter, not for the sake of your family or your friends, but for the sake of finding God, won't you consider reading His book?

From start to finish, this sixty-six-book epic romance is the story of God's lavish love. It's all in there for you to discover—if you're willing to open it up and read it through. Don't try to understand the entirety of God's love by reading bits and pieces of His love letter. Similarly, if you want to love Him back with your whole heart, His whole book will teach you how!

The opening words are, "In the beginning," and the benediction concludes with an emphatic "Amen." But it's more than a story; it is life to those who believe. The Bible isn't just a sweeping narrative we attempt to apply to our lives; it is our very life.

The wisdom of Proverbs is that God's words "are life to those who find them" (4:22). *Life.* Not merely the secret to a good life, but life itself. Of course, our lives, practically speaking, are much too busy to try to figure out what that even means. Except we must. You must. You must purpose in your heart and throughout your busy days to understand how God's Word speaks into every fiber of your life. Seek to understand that and you will.

While I loved reading my Bible as a girl, I never considered reading it from cover to cover until I was twenty-seven years old. It was in the Bible study I had joined as a newlywed that I received the invitation I must have been waiting for. After going through a few Bible studies together, an older woman who had joined our group as a mentor suggested that we actually read the Bible itself.

Ann Bentley was her name. I'll never forget her or the other women in that little weekly study. Ann knew our lives would only get busier once we started growing our families. She challenged us with words I am eager to pass on to you now: "If you have not yet read the Bible that you say you believe, how much do you actually believe it?"

Submit to seeking, then feast on what you find.

What a convicting, uncomfortable thought. But also, what an incredible opportunity to encounter more of God than we'd ever thought to encounter before. I'm so glad I said yes to her invitation. Today I'm asking you to say yes too. If you have not yet read the Bible that you say you believe, how much do you actually believe it? **If you say the Bible story is your story, then read the story and allow it to shape the remaining chapters of your life.** For these words are *life* to those who find them!

Therefore, do not casually consume God's life-giving message in bits and pieces here and there. If it truly offers to save your life, transform your life, bring healing and direction to your life, and *be your very life*, then intentionally sit down daily and ingest it as a life-sustaining sixty-six-course feast. Open it up and find out how one course is extravagantly followed by the next. Take the words of the Father and eat them, taste them and see them, believe and confess them. Allow each morsel to shape and transform you as you read. Submit to seeking, then feast on what you find.

If you believe the Bible is God's Word, spoken to you, but you have not read it through, now is the time. If you would bet your eternal life on God's Word, spend some of your present life reading it.

Grandpa read it four times before he believed, and yet most Christ followers who have believed have not read it through even one time. Since I am now the "older woman" in many Bible study circles today, allow me to personally invite you to seek God in the entirety of His Word, from Genesis to Revelation!

Lord, I'm open to opening Your Word and reading it through. I am. Holy Spirit, give me direction and courage and perhaps some friends to join me on the journey. I want to know all of You, and I realize today that reading all of Your Words will help me to do just that. I pray this in the name of the One who is the complete Word of God—Jesus, Amen.

THE FEAST

Proverbs 2
Proverbs 4

FOOD FOR THOUGHT

Consider today's challenge. Whether you have read your Bible the whole way through before or not, would you be willing to read it from beginning to end? Who might you invite to join you on your journey?

The first time I read through the Bible, I did so with a group. We completed it in 365 days, and it changed all the days that came after for each and every one of us. The next time I journeyed through those same pages, it took me four years! Ann Bentley was right, my life got busier once I started having babies. Now that those babies are grown, I'm still choosing, actively and obediently, to read it over and over again. Sometimes I go quickly through the books, other times I savor them slowly. Find a Bible reading plan that fits your season, then invite some friends to join you! If you need some help getting started, I've provided three different Bible reading plans at wendyspeake.com/feast.

day 25

THE GOSPELS

Jesus did many other things as well. If every one of them were written down, I suppose that even the whole world would not have room for the books that would be written.

John 21:25

DURING THE MONTH OF DECEMBER each year, I like to read through the book of Matthew. Wherever I find myself in my personal Bible reading at the time, I typically press pause and dive into this first Gospel account of Jesus's life, death, and resurrection. Since there are only twenty-eight chapters in Matthew, it's easy to make this a simple and special tradition that extends through the holiday season. Reading about Jesus's birth as I decorate our tree helps me prepare my heart as I prepare my home.

If you tend to get distracted by the shopping and wrapping, the baking and busyness, this Bible reading practice may help you keep your focus on the Christ child of Christmas. It's also a very simple way to invite your family and friends to join you in God's Word during the holidays.

However, consider yourself warned: once you finish the book of Matthew, you may be tempted to move right on into Mark, then Luke, and finally, the Gospel account of John. Depending on where Easter falls on the calendar that year, and how many chapters you've read each day, you'll likely wrap up the Gospels around Resurrection Sunday. The timing is perfect! Four times in a row, you'll have read about the life, death, and resurrection of Jesus.

Of course, there's no need to wait until Christmas. You can start anytime.

Perhaps you're intrigued and eager to give it a try. Or maybe you're confused, wondering, *Why would you read four different versions of the same story, and what would possess you to do it year after year?*

Most of us typically don't read the same story again and again once we know the ending. However, where the gospel is concerned, it is our knowledge of the story's end that keeps us coming back for more! Every year on Good Friday I wear a T-shirt that says, "Spoiler Alert: The Tomb Is Empty!" The fact that we know the end doesn't keep us from celebrating the beginning. Quite the contrary. It's because of Christ's resurrection that we return to the story of His birth.

Over and over, again and again, we begin at the beginning, remembering that God sent His Son to chase us down in our sin and separation. That's where the good news starts. Emmanuel, God with us, the Word wrapped in flesh was born for us. Once He was born, however, Jesus had to grow up, and reading the Gospels allows us to tag along so that we might grow up too. The Gospel account doesn't merely bring us to faith, it matures our faith each time we revisit it.

Of course, the Gospel stories highlight only some of the things Jesus did and said. They are but a sampling of His wonder-working power—a small glimpse into His tender love for humanity. If all the lessons He faithfully lived and tirelessly taught were recorded, the world could not contain them. As it is, our hearts barely begin to understand what we know about Jesus. That's why we must return to the Gospels and hear Him teach the same lessons, time and again. As we do, we can encounter the reality of Jesus throughout every growing-up season of our lives.

While His forgiveness might be a one-and-done gift, the gift of growing up as a forgiven child of God takes a lifetime. Each time you read the Gospel accounts of those who walked with Him, you get to walk with Him too. As you witness the same old miraculous healings, they'll miraculously become new! And when you read for the umpteenth time how He was crucified in your place, you will find that your place is on your knees before Him—more receptive and responsive than ever before because you see, more clearly than ever, that the written account of God's demonstrative love is actually a demonstration of His love for you!

We will never finish learning to surrender to His love.

Although Jesus's last loving breath promised, "It is finished," we will never finish learning to surrender to His love (John 19:30). **We are never done learning to love Him back.** Growing up in our love for Him requires keeping our eyes on Christ. That's what reading and rereading the Gospels enables us to do—keep our eyes on Him.

A day is fast approaching when Jesus will come again to this earth. We are encouraged to keep our eyes on the skies, in eager anticipation of His return (1 Thess. 4:16–17). But how will we recognize Him as Lord when He comes again if we are not familiar with the story of His first coming? Reading the story of Jesus's life on earth and all it entailed is how we get ready for His return.

Jesus once told a sobering parable to demonstrate how we should all eagerly anticipate and prepare for that day. In the parable found in Matthew 25, we learn that ten virgins took their lamps out one night, waiting for a bridegroom to arrive for his wedding banquet. Once the sun went down, the virgins fell asleep. Sometime later, in the dead of night, they awoke to a loud cry: "Here's the bridegroom! Come out and meet him!" (v. 6).

The young women stood to their feet and prepared the wicks of their lamps, but only five had oil to light their way. The foolish ones begged the prepared ones to share their oil, but there wasn't enough to go around. So the women without oil stumbled back to town to find a merchant to sell them oil for their lamps. By the time they returned, the bridegroom was gone. The wise virgins had gone with him into the wedding banquet, and the door was shut behind them.

The late arrivals pounded on the door, asking to be let in. But the groom turned them away with the words, "I don't know you" (v. 12). At the tail end of that sobering story, Jesus warns us to keep watch, because we do not know the day or the hour of His return.

This idea of being ready for Christ's second coming is an excellent reason to keep turning and returning to the Gospels. We're told to keep watch, but how will we recognize Christ if we don't know what He looks like? And how will we know what He looks like if we don't have our eyes on Him? The Gospels enable us to keep our eyes on the Bridegroom.

Returning to the intimate, firsthand accounts of Christ's life and the lessons He taught is like storing up oil for your lamp. And learning to live as He lived, serving and sacrificing, healing and helping, is how you actively trim your wick.

If you've never read through the Gospels, what are you waiting for? And if you have read them, why not read them again? That's the thing about the Gospels, they never get old. Even as we grow old, they always apply.

Lord, help me to keep my eyes on You as I keep them on the pages of Matthew, Mark, Luke, and John. Each time I return to the same story, Your story, open my eyes to see new things, open my ears to hear Your voice in new ways, open my mind to understand Your stories and Your lessons better than I did the last time I read them, open my heart to experience Your love, and tender my will to love You back. In the name of the Bridegroom, I pray, because I long to be found ready, Amen.

THE FEAST

John 14

FOOD FOR THOUGHT

During today's Bible reading, ask yourself:

- What did I learn about God?
- What did I learn about myself?
- How do I need to live differently as a result?

Jesus repeatedly promised His disciples that He would return. If you knew Jesus was coming back one year from today, what would need to change in your life for you to be ready for Him?

day 26

THE LETTERS

If you love me, you will keep my commandments. And I will ask the
Father, and he will give you another Helper, to be with you forever.

John 14:15–16 ESV

I WAS TWELVE YEARS OLD, standing in the chapel at church
camp, singing all the familiar songs I had learned over the years,
when one lyric suddenly felt off. The words I had been singing
were, "If it cost me everything, I'll obey."[1]

I was your typical preteen and often sang the songs of my faith
with all my feelings while forgetting to engage my intellect. But
during that song it occurred to me, "I'm only twelve years old!
Am I really telling God that I'll obey Him, even if it costs me
everything? I don't even know what *everything* means." At that
moment, I closed my eyes and decided not to sing another word
unless I sincerely meant it. Standing there, I silently searched my
heart about my commitment to follow God regardless of what I
might have to give up along the way. As I wrestled with the con-
cept of complete surrender, I felt two hands upon my shoulders,
then a gentle yet firm pressure pushed me down into my chair.

Assuming that my camp counselor was behind me and noticed that I needed a quiet moment with the Lord, I submitted to their touch and sat down. I really did want to sing the song, so I asked the Lord to help me work through this issue *quickly*, before the last chorus. And He did.

As we neared the end of the final chorus, I opened my eyes, stood up, and sang out loud, "If it costs me everything, I'll obey." When the song ended, I turned around to share a smile with my counselor only to find that no one was seated behind me. It occurred to me, even at the age of twelve, that I had just experienced the Holy Spirit, the ultimate Counselor.

Today's Scripture from John 14 refers to the Holy Spirit as our "Helper." However, that same word can also be translated as "Counselor": "And I will ask the Father, and he will give you another Counselor to be with you forever" (v. 16 CSB). Though I turned around to look for my camp counselor that evening, it was the Holy Counselor who had helped me along in my faith. Thirty-five years later, I need the counsel of God's Spirit more than ever. As I read the Word, I need His help so that I don't read it mindlessly, but mindfully. And ultimately, I need His counsel if the Word I love is to shape the way I live.

Over the last couple of devotions, we've focused on where to begin reading your Bible. Today I'd like to suggest the Epistles! The word *epistle* is the Greek word for "letter." These are the letters the Holy Spirit breathed through the apostles and sent to the early churches. Just yesterday I encouraged you to read Matthew, Mark, Luke, and John, then mentioned that the story continues after Jesus's resurrection. When you wrap up the Gospels, you'll come to the book of Acts, which documents the dramatic and explosive growth of the early church. Immediately after that action-packed book, you'll arrive at these letters, the Epistles.

While the Holy Spirit inspired the whole Bible, His role as our Counselor is perhaps most helpful as we read the Epistles. Sure, we need the gentle pressure of the Spirit to help us understand that Jesus is the Son of God, but it's the Counselor's conviction that causes us to be transformed into the image of God as we learn to live like it's true. In the Gospels, we learn that Jesus was nailed to the cross, but it's in the Epistles that we're told why and then counseled on how to live as a result. Jesus came to forgive our sins, and the Holy Spirit helps us to stop sinning.

The letters to the early churches are packed full of instructions regarding how we are to live. Since we have been made right, we need to know how to live right! Because we are no longer slaves to sin, we need to know how to live free. These letters, along with the ongoing help of the Helper, are the key.

In his letter to the Galatians, the apostle Paul wrote, "I have been crucified with Christ and I no longer live, but Christ lives in me. The life I now live in the body, I live by faith in the Son of God, who loved me and gave himself for me" (2:20).

Since we have been made right, we need to know how to live right!

Though the words were breathed by God, they were penned by Paul, who also wrote these words to the start-up church in Rome: "For we know that our old self was crucified with him so that the body ruled by sin might be done away with, that we should no longer be slaves to sin— because anyone who has died has been set free from sin" (6:6–7).

The letters to the churches are letters to each of us, reminding us that we have a choice to make. If Christ died for our sins, crucifying them on the cross, burying them in the grave, and leaving them there when He rose again, then we must learn to live like it's true. We must make the choice to let Christ—not sin—motivate our life now. After all, it's no longer us living, following through on each sinful impulse, but Christ living and moving and having His way in us—for His glory, our greatest good, and the benefit of those around us.

Miraculously, over time, the more we humbly accept the love of God through the Word of God, the less prone we are to keep on sinning. Likewise, the more we believe that Christ nailed our sins to the cross, the more our desire to sin diminishes. When Christ, rather than sin, rules on the throne of our lives, our lives naturally begin to transform into His image rather than our old image.

In his letter to the Colossians, Paul wrote:

> Since, then, you have been raised with Christ, set your hearts on things above, where Christ is, seated at the right hand of God. Set your minds on things above, not on earthly things. For you died, and your life is now hidden with Christ in God. When Christ, who is your life, appears, then you also will appear with him in glory.
>
> Put to death, therefore, whatever belongs to your earthly nature. (3:1–5)

These apostolic excerpts are full of nitty-gritty application when considering our old sin-stained struggles, but they are also packed full of celebratory hope. Though the transformation process isn't easy, Jesus didn't leave us alone to figure it out. He gave us His Holy Spirit to help us read and apply each letter to our lives. Jesus saved us, but His Holy Spirit helps us to celebrate our salvation and live saved, He counsels us to live forgiven since we've been forgiven, He guides us to live right since we've been made right with God, He enables us to live holy since we are wholly loved, and He helps us to live as though our sins are no longer leading us, because they aren't—He is. The Spirit of God leads us, helps us, counsels us, and guides us.

This is the marriage that leads to the Christian's transformation: the Word of God coupled with the Spirit of God transforms us into the image of God.

Author and pastor Nate Pickowicz said it this way, "The Bible is powerful and able to change your life from the inside out. No other means is given by God to accomplish such a task. The Spirit of God, who is at work in the hearts of Christians, uses the Word of God to transform them into Christlike people."[2]

Throughout your Christian life, make sure to sit down regularly at the table of your personal Bible study with the Holy Spirit and feast on the Epistles with Him. Ingest them slowly, as though they were written to you, because they were. Allow the Spirit to gently apply pressure and pin you to your seat as you consider the words: "I have been crucified with Christ and I no longer live, but

Christ lives in me" (Gal. 2:20). When you are ready to claim Paul's declaration as your own, stand up and sing.

> *Holy Spirit, help me to live like Your inspired Word is true. Counsel and guide me. I pray in Jesus's name, Amen.*

THE FEAST

Romans 6

FOOD FOR THOUGHT

Invite the Lord to pin you to your seat with Romans 6 so that you might pinpoint one dead-to-sin part of your life that you keep trying to resurrect. Then ask the Helper to help you lay it down for good.

day 27

LEARN TO LINGER

Oh, how I love your law!
I meditate on it all day long.

Psalm 119:97

IN THE SUMMER OF 2018, I traveled to Israel with a small group of authors and Bible teachers. As we drove from location to location, our tour guide had us read Bible passages aloud over the bus intercom, preparing us for what we would encounter next. Almost every time one of us would start to read, our guide would take one hand off the steering wheel, wave it in the air, and yell, "Slowly, read it slowly!"

Startled, the reader would start over from the beginning, only to be interrupted again. Gently applying his foot to the brakes for added emphasis, and slowing his own words too, the guide repeated, "Slowly, read it slowly."

For ten days we hurried from site to site, morning to night, hustling to see as much as we possibly could. But when it came time to read God's Word, we learned to slow our pace and read each word as though it truly was *breathed by God*. Because it was.

Perhaps that's why visiting the Holy Land is a breathtaking experience—it's where the story was breathed. While each biblical story seemed to come to life before my eyes in Israel, learning to slow down when reading my Bible on a daily basis has allowed God's Word to come alive wherever I am. I never knew the power of slowly reading through familiar passages until that trip. Learning to slow down when reading God's Word is one of the main Bible study skills I hope to pass on to you through these feasting days. Slow the actual cadence of your Bible reading, then slow down further and learn to linger longer.

Most Christians who spend time in their Bibles don't spend much time there at all. I don't mention this to condemn those who read quickly, but to encourage a slower pace. We have ample time to scroll through social media and consume newsreels each day. We binge-watch shows on Netflix, but we hurry through our quiet time with the Lord.

We gobble up His presence and gobble up His Word as if we're in a rush. Brushing the crumbs from our lap, we stand up and move on with more indigestion than transformation and wonder why we don't look more like Him. One pastor put it this way, "Reading the Bible without meditating on it is like eating without chewing."[1]

If we liken our Bible reading to an actual meal, I'd say we often look for nutrients to keep us alive while missing out on the flavor that makes life worth living. However, meditating on the feast that is God's Word, sitting with Christ at the table, and learning from His Spirit, allows us to do more than simply receive a spiritual IV drip; we get to taste the sweetness of our Savior and the flavor of His friendship.

When we slow down to sit with Him and learn from Him, meditating on the message He came to bring, we are transformed by both the message and the Messenger. As we savor the way His commandments were intended to protect us and linger over the way He leads us through each valley, calling us up to high places, our reading becomes richer. And the sweeter our Bible reading gets, the sweeter the Lord Himself is to us.

I'm reminded, yet again, of the verse I shared in the introduction to our forty-day feast: "Taste and see that the LORD is good" (Ps. 34:8). Gulping His goodness by gulping down the good news doesn't allow us to taste and see it for ourselves. That's why we've got to learn to slow down and savor. Just as we can read our Bibles and rush right by the God of the Bible, it's possible to read God's Word and never taste how good it is. But when we learn to linger and start to savor, there's a greater chance we will catch the flavor of His goodness.

It's possible to read God's Word and never taste how good it is.

Perhaps this is the secret to an abundant life. Many believe in eternal life through faith in Christ and ingest their Bibles to get there, but they miss out on the feast of living. **Don't simply read your Bible to get to heaven tomorrow; allow the Word to bring a taste of heaven into your life today.**

I love how author David Mathis says it in his book *Habits of Grace*: "Don't let the push to check boxes keep you from lingering over a text, whether to seek to understand it ('study') or to emotionally glory in what you understand ('meditation')."[2]

I want to learn to linger, and I want you to learn it with me. Let's not read the Scriptures with hurried hearts as we hustle through our days. Let's learn to linger, to meditate on the Word of God, ingest it carefully, and digest it fully, so we can "emotionally glory" in what we understand.

If you want to enjoy the Bible's flavor, you have to learn to savor. Here are three practical ways to meditate on the Scriptures throughout the day:

- *Slowly, read it slowly.* Don't read the Word faster than you can understand it. It is better to read less of the Bible and understand it more than it is to gulp down large servings without tasting a thing.

- *Write it down and take it with you.* Sometimes I write down a key verse on an index card, then fold it up and tuck it into my purse or pocket. Like leftovers from a wonderful feast, I am able to take the card out and enjoy it later in the day.

- *Read it again.* Many mornings, I open my Bible to continue my reading only to have the previous day's passage (along with the notes I left in the margin) pull me back to the very same lesson. On those days, I know deep down that I'm not ready to move on yet. So I read the same passage again. Sometimes I stay in one chapter for a long string of days, unable to turn the page. It's as though that one Bible story, life lesson, facet of God's goodness, or deep conviction pins me there and doesn't allow me to move on until I can move on changed.

But perhaps none of these practices will make any sense at all until we learn to love God's Word. The psalmist proclaimed, "Oh, how I love your law! I meditate on it all day long" (Ps. 119:97). **If you don't yet love God's Word, you won't love reading it. However, as you learn to love the flavor, it will become a delight to savor.** Today the feast portion of your reading is short and sweet. Linger over it a time or two, then write the last two verses down on a slip of paper to snack on throughout your day.

Learning to linger over God's Word is what makes the difference between simply surviving—receiving nutrients through an IV—and thriving by feasting on flavorful foods, slowly savoring each morsel, bringing goodness to your taste buds and joy to your life.

Lord, I long to linger. Help me to stay in Your presence as I stay in Your Word, without rushing off. Teach me to read it slowly and then carry it with me throughout my days. And most of all, Lord, help me to love Your Word. Because I love You, I ask all this in the sweet, sweet name of Jesus, Amen.

THE FEAST

Psalm 119:41–48

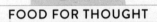

FOOD FOR THOUGHT

Notice how love is mentioned at both the beginning and the end of this short passage. God's love for us, demonstrated through His salvation, should lead us to a demonstrative love response.

How would you characterize your love of God's Word in this season of your life?

day 28

CHEW THE CUD

> Blessed is the one
> who does not walk in step with the wicked
> or stand in the way that sinners take
> or sit in the company of mockers,
> but whose delight is in the law of the LORD,
> and who meditates on his law day and night.
>
> Psalm 1:1–2

I WANT TO LINGER a little longer on yesterday's lesson to make sure we get everything out of it before hustling on to another idea. Choosing to camp out on many of the same Scriptures for a second time is the perfect picture of what meditating on God's Word often looks like.

I'm reminded of the way a cow chews its cud. I used to think that cud was another word for food or grass, but it's not. Cud refers to the partially digested food that has been returned to the cow's mouth for further chewing. A cow's stomach has four compartments. Once a cow chews its food for a short while, the grass is sent down to the first cavity to break down with the help of digestive enzymes. After that, the food is sent back up to the cow's mouth for a second round of slow chewing before it is passed down to the second stomach compartment, where the remaining nutrients are extracted from it.[1] Today we are chewing the cud from yesterday as we further digest the idea of meditating on God's Word to get all the nutrients out of it.

In today's verse you read that the blessed man does not walk in the counsel of the wicked, nor does he stand in the way of sinners or sit in the seat of scoffers. Instead, he delights in the law of the Lord, and on His law, he meditates *all day and night.* A blessed person seeks counsel from God, first and foremost. Basically, those who are blessed and set apart "chew the cud" with Him.

Those who are blessed don't rush through God's Word then hustle out the front door. Instead, they set their minds intentionally on God's counsel and keep talking it through with their heavenly Counselor. Walking and talking—morning, noon, and nighttime—they go through life with God as their guide.

Here's another passage to chew on as we consider how meditating on God's Word is key to a blessed life:

> Do not merely listen to the word, and so deceive yourselves. Do what it says. Anyone who listens to the word but does not do what it says is like someone who looks at his face in a mirror and, after looking at himself, goes away and immediately forgets what he looks like. But whoever looks intently into the perfect law that gives freedom, and continues in it—not forgetting what they have heard, but doing it—they will be blessed in what they do. (James 1:22–25)

Years ago I memorized just a snippet of this passage: "Do not merely listen to the word and so deceive yourselves. Do what it says." While that short command is worthy of hiding in your heart, on its own it doesn't communicate the heart of God. His intent isn't to demand submission but to extend blessing to those who submit. The invitation is clear: Read and continue reading, obey and keep obeying, and you will be blessed. God's Word is a road map to the blessed life! Though God's boundaries may sometimes feel like restrictions holding you back from the good life, His commandments are guardrails keeping you safe on your way to the best life! Love is at the core of each command. Love is at the center, the very crux of every jot and tittle.

As you chew the cud each day, resist the temptation to extract knowledge without receiving the blessing of knowing and trusting God. Knowing, trusting, and ultimately obeying Him leads to a long life of blessing! So slow down and meditate on what *Love is at the core* you read—both as you read it and after *of each command.* you're done reading. Keep in step with His clear counsel. Take your time to understand His Word, then prayerfully and carefully apply it to your life as you go about your day. Yes, walk it out with Him in metered steps by His loving side.

Charles Spurgeon once said, "We profit by the Word of God not through hasty reading, but through deep meditation."[2] And pastor Tim Keller wrote, "God's way is perfect and his Word is flawless. A perfect God could have nothing less than perfect communication with his people. It is we who read hastily, skip prayer, and fail to meditate on his Word, who find it confusing."[3] I would add that when we read it hastily, we don't just find it confusing, we also miss the blessing God intended.

Returning for a second portion is what meditating often looks like. Just as cows chew their cud to extract all the nutrients and dogs gnaw bones to get down to the marrow where the very best flavor resides, we can meditate on Scripture to get the most out of it. God's Word isn't what we need to merely get us through life, it is what leads us to the blessed life. In the deepest part of His communication with us, God has placed the key to life eternal and life abundant. Choose whichever metaphor you like—chewing the cud or gnawing on a bone—but don't move on and leave the counsel of God's Word behind. If you do, you'll eventually fall in step with the counsel of this world, and that doesn't lead to the same blessed destination.

Before you dive into today's feast, slowly read the passage below. See how beautifully it dovetails with Psalm 1 and our overarching theme of tasting the sweetness and goodness of God's Word as we read it for ourselves.

> Oh, how I love your law!
>> I meditate on it all day long.
> Your commands are always with me
>> and make me wiser than my enemies.
> I have more insight than all my teachers,
>> for I meditate on your statutes.
> I have more understanding than the elders,
>> for I obey your precepts.
> I have kept my feet from every evil path
>> so that I might obey your word.
> I have not departed from your laws,
>> for you yourself have taught me.
> How sweet are your words to my taste,
>> sweeter than honey to my mouth!
> I gain understanding from your precepts;
>> therefore I hate every wrong path. (Ps. 119:97–104)

Lord, thank You for speaking to me today through Your Word. Help me to slow down each time I read it, then prompt my heart to return to its meaning throughout my days. Seeking Your kind counsel rather than the world's wisdom will lead me to the blessed life and the sweet life. I believe that is true. I believe in You, and I believe in Your Word, Lord Jesus. Amen.

THE FEAST

Psalm 1

FOOD FOR THOUGHT

Based on what you read in Psalm 1, ask yourself these questions:

- What did I learn about God?
- What did I learn about myself?
- How do I need to live differently as a result?

day 29

KNOW IT BY HEART

I have hidden your word in my heart
that I might not sin against you.

Psalm 119:11

ONE OF MY SWEETEST MEMORIES as a mom is of my first-born son, Caleb, marching through Target on his way to the toy section. He swung his scrawny little arms and pumped his little-boy legs while singing a musical version of these verses penned by the apostle Paul: "The fruit of the Spirit is love, joy, peace, forbearance, kindness, goodness, faithfulness, gentleness, and self-control. . . . Since we live by the Spirit, let us keep in step with the Spirit" (Gal. 5:22–23, 25).

Though he was only three years old at the time, my boy took up my challenge to see how many Bible verses he could memorize. As an added incentive, I rewarded him with a small toy car each time he learned another verse. Of course, I had no idea at the time how easy the challenge would be for a preschooler who had a sponge-like brain. And I made it so easy for him! Everywhere we went, we listened to a CD of short Scripture songs. Over the course of that year, Caleb collected quite a few cars, thirty-three to be exact.

Of course, that means he stored thirty-three Bible verses in the memory tank of his heart as well.

It was in that same season that one day I took Caleb, his baby brother, and my pregnant belly to a local park for an afternoon of fun. As I pushed my second-born in the toddler swing, Caleb sat in the sand, digging beside a boy he had only just met. Apparently this other child did something (I don't remember what) that upset my boy. Caleb, obviously distraught and ready to retaliate, came to me, took a deep breath, and said, "Do not be overcome by evil, but overcome evil with good," then walked back to his shovel.

My jaw dropped. Romans 12:21 was one of the Scripture songs he had sung into the deep recesses of his being until it became his personal belief and his public behavior. What a perfect picture of Psalm 119:11. Caleb knew God's Word by heart. When sin threatened, the Word of God, hidden in his heart, held him back from doing wrong. God's Word spoke to Caleb from within his memory at the tender age of three. That was a defining moment for me as a mom and as a Bible-believing Christ follower myself. When we know God's Word by heart, God's Word gets hidden in our hearts and speaks truth to our deepest self when we're tempted to sin.

While I was writing this book, Caleb turned eighteen years old. Temptation looks different now than it did all those years ago. Today pornography is readily available at his fingertips, real-life girls would willingly "go too far," music and movies celebrating and encouraging immorality are streaming online, and addictive substances are sold at every gas station throughout the country. Just the other day he told me that he can count on one hand the friends he has who don't cuss. Temptation is at every turn, every day, day after day.

We may not be in the sandlot or on school campuses, but we are each tempted to sin. We are tempted to give up when we grow weary, to hold grudges rather than forgive. We are tempted to drown our sorrows with alcohol rather than seek the comfort God offers and to find our identity beyond Christ rather than in Him. We are tempted to be boastful, to gossip, and to be fearful. Yes, we are all tempted—and that's why this lesson is for us.

When we know God's Word by heart, God's Word holds us by the heart. Tethered to His heart, He holds us back from sin. Conversely, when we are not bridled by the Bible or controlled by the Spirit, we are wildly uncontrolled—and that doesn't lead us to the blessed life on which we meditated yesterday. The blessed life is outlined in the Bible, where God graciously invites us to obey each of His loving instructions. Little Caleb needed and heeded those instructions at three, but he needs them more than ever at eighteen. We all need them, regardless of our age or life stage. God has given us His Word for such a time as this. The lamplight of God's Word applies to these dark days. **It is the light source we need to help us live right when the world lives wrong.**

The lamplight of God's Word applies to these dark days.

I'm reminded of the clear command God gave to Israel through Moses when He told them, "Place The Testimony that I give you in the Chest" (Exod. 25:16 MSG). In context, God was talking about placing the Ten Commandments inside the chest that was the ark of the covenant. But within the context of your life, remember to place God's Word deep in your "chest"—down deep in your heart.

In yesterday's devotion we learned that when we meditate on God's Word throughout the day, we'll be more likely to obey throughout the day. Likewise, when we hide His Word in our heart, we are far less likely to disobey. So take the verses you are meditating on one step further and memorize them too. We don't want to simply avoid temptation for one day, but for all the days of our lives.

The psalmist challenges us, "How can a young man keep his way pure? By keeping it according to Your word" (Ps. 119:9 NASB). While I love that translation, I have encouraged Caleb and his brothers to consider this translation of the same verse as they grow into young men: "How can a young man keep his way pure? By guarding it according to your word" (ESV). The word "guarding" is more muscular—it's a stronger word for my strong-willed sons. But, again, this admonition isn't just for young men but for us all, because we all need to get more muscular in our faith lives.

How can we actively obey and experience the blessed life God has for us if we don't remember what God has instructed us to do or what he has warned us not to do? **We must get into our Bibles to the point that our Bibles get into us.** We must memorize His Word daily so that He might speak to us during our daily lives. If Bible memorization is a new spiritual discipline for you, don't be afraid to start small. Today's verse is just fifteen words: "I have hidden your word in my heart that I might not sin against you" (Ps. 119:11).

Starting small is big.

Each time I'm tempted to look down on small starts and small steps toward obedience, I'm reminded of these words from the prophet Zechariah, "Do not despise these small beginnings, for the LORD rejoices to see the work begin" (4:10 NLT).

Dear Lord, I'm ready to start. Guide me to the verse that You want me to know by heart and I will hide it in my heart today. I can't wait to hear You speaking to me from deep within my chest when temptation comes my way. From my heart to Yours, in Jesus's name I pray, Amen.

THE FEAST

Psalm 119:1–24

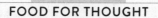

FOOD FOR THOUGHT

As you feast on the first few sections of Psalm 119, be on the lookout for a short verse or a longer passage you want to commit to memory. And don't forget to dig deep with these questions:

- What did I learn about God?
- What did I learn about myself?
- How do I need to live differently as a result?

day 30

HEARING GOD'S VOICE

My sheep hear my voice, and I know them, and they follow me.

John 10:27 ESV

THE LITTLE BOY I MENTIONED in yesterday's reading was born one week before Christmas 2003. The afternoon we brought him home from the hospital, I sat in a comfy chair by the fireplace memorizing my infant's face in the glow of twinkling Christmas tree lights. It was in that chair that I learned to nurse my son, giving him the food he needed to survive. It was also in that chair, on that very first day together in our home, that I looked over and saw my husband's Bible on the coffee table before me. Awkwardly, I shifted the babe in my arms and picked it up.

Somehow I knew that there was a sustenance even more nourishing than a mother's milk—a heavenly Father's love. So I opened the love letter and began to read it out loud, starting in Genesis 1. By New Year's Eve, my child and I were through the book of Genesis and into Exodus. Of course, my son wasn't learning lessons as I read aloud. He merely slept and nursed and slept some more.

But as he slept and as he nursed, his ears caught the cadence of God's voice. I believe that.

I've heard people say, "I just want to hear God speak out loud to me." I understand the heart of what they are saying—they want God to speak clearly into their circumstances, providing the answers they are looking for in some obvious way. Goodness, so do I! But each time I hear someone say that they want to hear God speak, I encourage them to read their Bibles out loud.

Evangelist Justin Peters once said, "Want to hear God speak? Read your Bible. Want to hear God speak audibly? Read your Bible out loud!"[1] Likewise, pastor Mark Batterson wrote, "When you open your Bible, God opens His mouth."[2]

With my newborn babe cradled in one arm and my husband's Bible balanced in the other, God opened His mouth and mother and son both heard Him speak. I don't recall how many chapters of how many books of the Bible I read aloud to baby Caleb, but by the time he could sleep through the night He had probably heard more verses than most people hear in a lifetime.

When that same child of mine was in the fourth grade and reading through a children's storybook Bible on his own, he came across the story of another young boy who heard God's voice. The child was Samuel, and God called to him during the night (1 Samuel 3). Multiple times during the night, Samuel rolled off his mat and woke up Eli the priest, thinking that it was Eli who had called him.

"No, I didn't call you, Samuel," the old man told the young boy over and over. Eventually, Eli realized that the child was hearing God's voice and told him to return to his bed. "If he calls you, say, 'Speak, Lord, for your servant is listening'" (v. 9).

Samuel returned to his mat and laid down once more. Eventually the Lord came and stood beside the child, calling as he had called him those other times, "Samuel! Samuel!"

Samuel was ready with his response, "Speak, for your servant is listening" (v. 10).

Caleb recounted this story back to me one day with wide eyes. He said, "That same thing happened to me." Then, turning to his dad, he said, "Don't you remember that time I kept coming to you thinking that you were calling me, but you weren't? It must have been God!"

I love that story with all my mothering heart, but it was another story of another voice that called out to Caleb on another night that taught me how important it is to know God's voice.

Caleb was still in elementary school and having a hard time sleeping. While tossing and turning through the night, he struggled with dark and anxious fears. Finally, he came to our room and quietly confessed, "I heard a voice, and it wasn't God's."

To this day, that story both frightens and comforts me in equal measure. For even though the Enemy is alive in our midst, roaming around us like the pompous prince of this earth, my son was able to distinguish his voice from God's. I have claimed John 10:27 over each one of my children since that night: "Lord, my children are Yours and You are theirs. Help them to know Your voice, that they might follow You all the days of their lives."

Those who know the Word of God are more likely to know the voice of God.

Today I am interceding for you as I write these words, praying that you, too, would know God's voice and follow Him, as a sheep follows a shepherd. And when the Enemy comes (for the Enemy most certainly will), I pray that you know him for who he is and say aloud a firm, "No, that's not God's voice!"

But how, you might ask, does one distinguish God's voice from the voice of this world's prince speaking this world's wisdom? Imprint the voice of truth on your heart and mind—actively, daily, morning by morning, and at nighttime too. Reading God's Word quietly gets it into your heart and mind, but reading it out loud gets it into your ears as well. That way, when falsehood speaks, both the message and the messenger can be denied. However, when the Spirit of God moves so clearly that you practically hear Him audibly, there will be no denying that message or the Messenger. Those who know the Word of God are more likely to know the voice of God.

If you have never read your Bible aloud, I invite you to try it today. During the feast portion of today's reading, open your Bible, then open your mouth and hear the Word of the Lord. Reading God's Word aloud engages your eyes, your mouth, and your ears—along with your heart and your mind.

Good Shepherd, I am Yours and You are mine. Help me to know Your voice and give me the courage to follow where You lead. In Jesus's name I pray, Amen.

THE FEAST

John 10
Psalm 95:1–7

FOOD FOR THOUGHT

I have a video of my youngest son reciting Psalm 95 when he was only seven. He had the most darling little voice and couldn't wrap his mouth around *r*'s yet. Still, when I replay that video and hear little Asher's voice reciting Scripture, I know I am hearing God speak.

Have you ever heard God speak in some supernatural way? If you have, enjoy the memory now. If you haven't, that's okay. Invite Him to speak supernaturally to you today, and in the meantime read His Word aloud.

day 31

TALK WITH YOUR MOUTH FULL

Pray without ceasing.

1 Thessalonians 5:17 ESV

I HAVE A BOOK that is nearly as tattered and worn from use as my Bible. My copy of Jodie Berndt's *Praying the Scriptures for Your Teens* is falling apart at the seams. Before I spent countless hours in these pages, however, I prayed my way through her first book, *Praying the Scriptures for Your Children*. Another well-worn book on my shelf, one I prayed my way through a few times before our first child was born, is Stormie Omartian's *The Power of a Praying Wife*. Are you noticing a theme here?

I love to pray God's Word.

It's a wonderful idea to pray before you eat literal food, but when it comes to a Bible feast, I'm also a fan of talking with your mouth full. When we ingest our Bibles, the conversation should continue long after we say Amen. Bible reading and prayer go hand in hand, especially when the words spoken to God are a response to God's words spoken to you.

In their books, both Jodie and Stormie chose multiple Scriptures that work together to cover a theme, such as God's will for humility in a marriage or for faith to take root in a child's heart. As they listed these verses, they left space for readers to insert the name of a child or spouse.

In recent years, I have taken to doing the same thing on my own. As I read the Word, I respond by praying God's words back to Him. Sometimes I pray whole passages over my children as blessings. Other times, I lift up verses and personalize them for my husband. Then there are Scriptures I lift to the Lord on my own behalf.

On day 28, we meditated on Psalm 1 together. That's one of my favorite passages to pray over my kids:

> *Lord, I pray that Caleb does not walk in the counsel of the wicked, nor stand in the way of sinners, nor sit in the seat of scoffers. I pray that his delight is in Your law and that he would meditate on Your law day and night. Then he will be like a tree firmly planted by streams of water that yields its fruit in its season. Its leaf does not wither. And in all that Caleb does, I pray that he prospers.*

Sometimes, when one of my loved ones is struggling to believe or behave, I bring that struggle to the Lord in the context of His Word. I remind Him, *Lord, Your Word says that You can replace hearts of stone with hearts of flesh (Ezek. 36:26). My child has a hard heart right now, and I'm asking You to soften it. If You were able to soften the heart of Pharaoh, You can surely soften my child's heart.*

Other times, I'm merely reading through the Word when I find myself inspired to pray for the godly traits I see in Bible characters such as Esther and David. After ingesting Bible stories, I serve them right back to God: *Lord, give me the courage that Esther had to obey You even when it's dangerous. Show me what that looks like in my world today, because You've put me here for such a time as this (Esther 4:14).*

Or, *Father, I ask that You grow our sons up into men who pursue Your heart, like King David (1 Sam. 13:14). Help them to learn skills, be brave, communicate clearly, and present themselves well. But above all, Lord, be with them (1 Sam. 16:18).*

The letters to the early churches are easy to personalize and pray back to the Lord as well: *Lord, I rejoice in You always. Let Your gentleness be evident—You are near. Therefore, I won't be anxious about anything, but in everything, through prayer and petition, with thanksgiving in my heart, I will present my requests to You. May Your peace, which transcends my understanding, guard my heart and mind in Christ Jesus. Help me, Lord, to think about things that are true, noble, right, and pure. Whatever is lovely, admirable, excellent, and praiseworthy—help me to fix my mind on such things. And Your peace will be with me! This is why I can rejoice (Phil. 4:4–9).*

I believe that Scripture-inspired prayers leave a legacy of faith within families for generations to come. As a matter of fact, I have three journaling Bibles with wide margins so I can jot down personalized Scripture prayers for each of them. I call these my Legacy Bibles and imagine what a treasure they will one day be for our sons.

Of course, you don't need to buy Bibles and write out prayers to leave a legacy of faith. Simply talk to God on behalf of those you know and love. As you feast on His Word, reply. Remind God of what He has spoken and tell Him that you believe it to be true. Declare your faith in His declarations. Agree with Him as you read with Him.

> Don't just pray before you eat, pray your way through the whole meal.

Don't just pray before you eat, pray your way through the whole meal. This is the only time it's completely appropriate to talk with your mouth full. God talks to you, and you listen. Praise Him for being such a kind communicator. Then ask Him questions as if you were face-to-face with the very best Bible teacher ever!

In the opening pages of one of Jodie Berndt's books, Mark Batterson wrote, "Scripture is God's way of initiating a conversation; prayer is our response."[1] Likewise, Eugene Peterson wrote in his book *Answering God*, "God speaks to us; our answers are our prayers. . . . Prayer by its very nature is answering speech."[2] And Charles Spurgeon once said, "When asked, 'What is more important: prayer or reading the Bible?' I ask, 'What is more important: breathing in or breathing out?'"[3]

God talks with us through our study of the Bible, but He's not a monologuing God. He's always been a relational God, and true to His nature, He invites us into a dialogue. We listen and we learn, we ask Him questions and listen to His answers. We seek those answers quietly through mediation because that's when God whispers. But sometimes He likes to shout, so we search for His answers in the Scriptures too. We listen and we learn some more, then admit our confusion and confess too. As we continue to read, he continues to communicate. Back and forth we dialogue.

In his book *Prayer*, Tim Keller wrote, "We speak only to the degree we are spoken to. . . . Our prayers should arise out of immersion in the Scripture. . . . This wedding of the Bible and prayer anchors your life down in the real God."[4] Similarly D. L. Moody said, "In our prayers we talk to God, in our Bible study God talks to us, and we had better let God do most of the talking."[5]

While I love good quotes about prayer, I would rather us get to the business of praying.

Lord, thank You for wanting to talk with me and hear from me too. It's amazing that You are so personal and available. I'm grateful. Please help me to take You up at Your invitation to talk with You without ceasing! I pray this in the available, dialoging name of Jesus, Amen.

THE FEAST

James 1

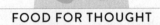

FOOD FOR THOUGHT

Take a few moments now to breathe out what you just breathed in as you read James 1. Respond to God's Word by praying it back to Him, for yourself or on behalf of your loved ones.

If you are inspired to pray God's Word over your children and grandchildren, consider creating a Legacy Bible. To learn more about the Legacy Bibles I am creating for my loved ones, visit wendyspeake.com/legacy-bibles.

day 32

A COMMENTARY ON COMMENTARIES

When they saw the courage of Peter and John and realized that they were unschooled, ordinary men, they were astonished and they took note that these men had been with Jesus.

Acts 4:13

EARLIER IN THIS MULTICOURSE FEAST, I invited you to read the Bible for yourself. I did not, however, tell you that you had to read it *by* yourself! As a matter of fact, back on day 18 I shared how powerful it was for me to engage with God in the Scriptures alongside a small community of Bible-believing friends. While we did our daily reading individually, we gathered corporately each week to share what we were learning. It was in this manner that we were able to learn beyond what we had learned on our own. God spoke to us individually, then He spoke through each individual in our community. As each person took their turn commenting on what they had learned from God, our comments became a living commentary.

Over the years, many authors and Bible scholars have written in-depth commentaries that provide literary bread crumbs for others to follow for greater understanding of the text. Bible commentaries communicate the overarching theme of each book of the Bible, explain the meaning of some original Hebrew and Greek words, include maps and timelines, and give insight into the historical context of each story.

On Sunday mornings, your pastor stands before you as a living, breathing commentary. The best preachers devote significant time combing through their Bibles as well as a stack of commentaries—like cooks searching for recipes to prepare a Sunday feast. Commentaries are a wonderful complement to Bible reading! If you need an additional resource to help you understand what you're reading, there are many to choose from. The goal isn't that you read the Bible by yourself, but that you read it.

The goal isn't that you read the Bible by yourself, but that you read it.

One of the most popular Christian podcasts today is Tara-Leigh Cobble's *The Bible Recap*. Each year thousands of men and women read through their Bibles alongside her. After completing the daily reading, listeners gain additional insights from Cobble's podcast, where she comments on the readings with context and backstory. At the end of each short episode, she zooms in on one theme. Each episode is only five to ten minutes long. *The Bible Recap* is also available in book form. Though my son and I are at vastly different seasons in our lives, we both enjoy listening to *The Bible Recap*.

While Cobble offers brief summaries of multiple chapters at a time, some written commentaries are wordier than the Bible itself! Over three hundred years ago, minister and scholar Matthew Henry compiled a six-volume set of commentaries that takes readers deep into God's Word. This resource continues to offer both pastors and laypeople a wide breadth of insight into the story and very nature of God. In the 1980s pastor and theologian J. Vernon McGee published *Thru the Bible*, a five-volume set that remains a popular commentary series today. And pastor John MacArthur's *The MacArthur Bible Commentary* offers brief explanations of every passage within one big book. As I type these words, Henrietta Mears's handbook *What the Bible Is All About* is beside me on my desk.

In the opening pages of our forty-day feast, I shared the story of my personal Bible collection. After I outgrew my little-girl Bible, my dad bought me a big-girl Bible. Each page of The Life Application Bible is divided into two parts: the top section is the Bible reading, and the bottom section comments on the passages above. This Bible, with its simple commentary, helped me understand the Bible for myself—though I wasn't actually reading it by myself. Others had left me notes, explaining the mystery of the Scriptures long before I opened them up.

As providence would have it, one of the editors of The Life Application Bible had been my dad's roommate at Wheaton College in the sixties. The fact that a family friend oversaw the creation of this commentary paints a beautiful picture. Within the family of God, pastors, authors, and other Bible-believing people have literally left us notes in our Bibles!

Similarly, I have learned to leave notes in the margins of my Bible. Long before I was a book writer, I was writing in God's book. My written comments over the years have become a very personal commentary, reminding me what God revealed to me the last time I was in that passage of study. My Bible notes chronicle my history with God in His Word. I'll circle a phrase, look up the original Hebrew or Greek word, and then write it down in the margin along with its definition. Other times, I'll simply insert another verse that I'm reminded of.

While many Bible teachers have had a formal education, never forget that God's Word is for ordinary men and women. Remember, Jesus's best friends were unschooled men. Acts 4:13 tells us, "When they saw the courage of Peter and John and realized that they were unschooled, ordinary men, they were astonished and they took note that these men had been with Jesus."

It was in the process of walking with Christ and talking with Christ that His followers became educated. They were taught by God, and we can be too.

Spending time with Jesus in the counsel of His Word provides the common woman with uncommon wisdom and the ordinary man with extraordinary understanding. The more you open your Bible and hear from Him, the more comfortable and confident you will become. Perhaps one day someone will listen to you comment on the Scriptures and think, *Wow! What courage and confidence they have.* Just like Peter and John, you might consider yourself unschooled and common, until you walk with our uncommon Savior.

Spend great gobs of time with Jesus in His Word, my friend, then spend time with others who have spent even more time with Him than you have. As you become wiser, add your comments to the conversation in Sunday School classes and midweek Bible studies at church. Read commentaries to deepen your understanding, then let your life become a living commentary as you invite others to join you in the Bible as well.

Yes, spend time with Jesus, and then spend time with people who have not been with Jesus so that they can spend time with Jesus through you. Allow your life to be a walking, talking testimony and a living commentary! When the ordinary woman and the common man walk with Jesus, they have the extraordinary privilege of walking with others so that they too might walk with God.

Jesus, thank You for providing me with people who have walked with You through the pages of Your Word longer than I have. With the help of Your Holy Spirit and their generous testimonies and shared wisdom, make me uncommonly wise so I might testify too. I long to comment on Your goodness to the next generation. I ask all of this in the noteworthy name of Jesus. Amen.

THE FEAST

Acts 4

FOOD FOR THOUGHT

Today's feast is rich with verses on which I would love to comment. However, I will focus in on just one. Let's consider it today's sweet dessert. Peter and John cried out, "As for us, we cannot help speaking about what we have seen and heard" (Acts 4:20). Oh, that their cry would be our life's commentary as well!

How comfortable do you feel sharing what you learn from God's Word with others? In what small way might you actively practice becoming a walking, talking testimony in the next twenty-four hours? Or, how might you seek out the biblical wisdom and insight of others? Either way, make a plan to engage in God's Word with another person today.

day 33

WHEN THE BIBLE IS CONFUSING

And beginning with Moses and with all the Prophets, [Jesus] explained to them what was said in all the Scriptures concerning himself.

Luke 24:27

MY SONS LOVE TO QUOTE MOVIE LINES back and forth. While I don't typically play the game aloud with them, there is one quote I think of often when reading my Bible. It was spoken by Forrest Gump to his beloved Jenny, "I'm not a smart man, but I know what love is."[1] That's how I sometimes feel when reading God's Word. Though I don't understand it all, I do know that it is a message of love.

Unfortunately, most people think they need to be super smart and already full of biblical knowledge to open up their Bibles and start reading. Because they're not yet as knowledgeable as they think they should be, they keep their Bibles closed. Of course, closing one's Bible only closes the door to growing in wisdom in the Word, so the cycle of ignorance continues, as does the ongoing confusion.

"I'm not a smart woman, but—" I know that one of the most common reasons why Bible-believing Christians aren't Bible-reading Christians is because they don't understand what they're reading. So that's why, on day 3 of our feast, I gave you a brief overview of the Bible narrative in its simplest form in an attempt to make it feel a little less daunting and a little more doable—a little more relatable and a little more readable. Then yesterday I suggested using a trusty commentary to help bring clarity when you're confused. Today, however, I want to suggest an even sweeter resource: Jesus Himself! Perhaps you're familiar with this verse from Luke 24: "And beginning with Moses and with all the Prophets, [Jesus] explained to them what was said in all the Scriptures concerning himself" (v. 27).

This verse comes from a passage often referred to as "On the Road to Emmaus." It takes place after the crucifixion but before all of Jesus's followers knew He had risen from the dead. Overwhelmed by grief and confusion, two of Jesus's followers left Jerusalem and were walking to Emmaus. They did not understand what was going on and were ready to close the metaphorical book they had been reading. Only they hadn't been reading about Jesus, they had actually been walking with Him and listening to Him.

When Jesus, the one they had believed to be the Messiah, had been crucified three days earlier, all their understanding evaporated into misunderstanding. The hope they had put in Him was nailed to the cross along with their teacher. In their confusion, they wandered away from the other followers. They were closing the book on their faith because it no longer made sense to them.

Jesus, in His kindness, chased them down and walked beside them as they questioned everything. Though they didn't recognize Him, Jesus explained again what the Scriptures said about the Messiah, starting at the very beginning. He showed them how all of the laws and all of the prophecies had been pointing to Him, promising His appearance. The two travelers had forgotten all these things in the shadow of His death. This is why Jesus, kind and articulate

Jesus, explained it again. And when He broke bread with them later that evening, they recognized Him at last and exclaimed, "Were not our hearts burning within us while he talked with us on the road and opened the Scriptures to us?" (Luke 24:32).

Jesus took time out of His very first resurrected day to chase down two men who walked away from the story before they got to the good part! Perhaps that's your tendency when it comes to God's Word. You stop reading because you do not understand. If so, before you beat yourself up, remember that these guys hadn't just read about Jesus, they had walked with Him as well. They had heard Him speak the truth aloud. I have to imagine that if God's grace extends to those who had every chance to hear and understand Jesus face-to-face, His gracious help must also extend to us, over two thousand confusing years later!

His gracious help must also extend to us.

Of course, those two weren't the only ones who struggled on that first Easter Sunday. Earlier that day, before Jesus walked along the dusty road to Emmaus, the women who loved Him most went to the tomb, fully expecting to find His body. When they arrived, however, their teacher wasn't there. In His place were two angelic men, whose attire "gleamed like lightning" (Luke 24:4). Frightened and confused, the women fell to their faces. When the angels spoke, they explained what had happened. Actually, they didn't explain much. They simply reminded the women what Jesus had already said, back in Galilee.

> "Why do you look for the living among the dead? He is not here; he has risen! *Remember how he told you*, while he was still with you in Galilee: 'The Son of Man must be delivered over to the hands of sinners, be crucified and on the third day be raised again.'" *Then they remembered his words.* (vv. 5–8, emphasis added)

Instead of meeting the women in their confusion and explaining everything to them again, Jesus simply sent angels to remind them of what He had already told them! Either way, it was Jesus, clearly communicating. And immediately after the ladies remembered everything Jesus Himself had clearly foretold, they went and shared the good news with the apostles. When the men heard what they had to share, however, "They did not believe the women, because their words seemed to them like nonsense" (v. 11).

Nonsense!

If you have ever felt that God's message sounded like nonsense, take heart! You're not the only one. Jesus's closest friends were confused and frustrated, but Jesus didn't leave them to figure things out alone. He met with them over the next forty days, serving up generous portions of clarifying words as He feasted with them over literal fires, roasting literal fish, and breaking literal bread. How kind He is!

And let's not forget Peter's response to the good news that the ladies brought back. Though the others heard nonsense, Peter "got up and ran to the tomb" (v. 12). He was eager to believe the unbelievable.

Here's what I hope you'll digest with me today. When we are confused about what we read in God's Holy Scriptures, there are three typical responses: fear, frustration, or fervor.

Fear. The women were afraid because they did not understand. When the angels appeared to them, they fell on their faces out of pure fright. However, once they calmed down and remembered what Jesus had already said, they were able to move forward with God's plan for them. Their fear had paralyzed them, but God had further plans for them!

Frustration. Most of Jesus's disciples weren't only afraid, holed up in a room together in Jerusalem, and fearful for their own lives, they were also frustrated. Like the travelers on the road to Emmaus, the disciples were ready to close the book because the story made no sense. But God, in His clarifying kindness, sent them the good news of Jesus's resurrection. And to the men on the road, He met them Himself. Jesus's flesh-and-blood appearance testified, "The story's not over!"

Fervor. Though Peter did not understand what the women reported, he was ready to jump up and believe. I imagine that down deep in his bones he knew there was more to the story. As soon as Mary pointed him in the right direction, Peter was off and running!

My dear feasting friend, you don't need to be a smart man or woman to know that God, in His loving-kindness, is wanting and waiting to communicate with you today. Jesus helps us understand His Word when we read it. **As we ingest the Bible, Christ helps us digest it too.** Bring your confusion and your questions to the One who walks with us and talks with us through His living Word and Holy Spirit.

Lord Jesus, when I don't understand Your Word or Your ways— my Bible or how to live it out—remind me what is true. I pray this simple prayer in the name of the kind and clear communicator, Jesus Christ, Amen.

THE FEAST

Luke 24

FOOD FOR THOUGHT

How do you tend to respond when you are confused? Do you shut out God and shut your Bible too? Or do you remain open to God and His Word? What about when His ways are not your ways? Are you more likely to react in fear, out of frustration, or with faithful fervor?

day 34

ON THE TABLE

The Lord Jesus, on the night he was betrayed, took bread, and when he had given thanks, he broke it and said, "This is my body, which is for you; do this in remembrance of me." In the same way, after supper he took the cup, saying, "This cup is the new covenant in my blood; do this, whenever you drink it, in remembrance of me."

1 Corinthians 11:23–25

THE LAST THING JESUS DID with his closest friends before He went to the cross was break bread with them around a table. However, that Last Supper wasn't His final feast. In yesterday's reading, you may have noticed that Jesus ended His first resurrected day by dining with His disciples again. Breaking bread was the last thing they did together before He laid down His life and the first thing they did together once He picked it back up.

Remember, feasting was God's idea from the start. He planned it, He planted it, and then He created us and invited us to the table. Perhaps that's why He peppered the pages of our Bibles with stories of feasts. The Old Testament book of Leviticus outlines weekly and annual celebratory meals to ensure that God's people would feast with Him regularly.

Of course, God's invitation to the feast isn't just for Jews. Today we'll look at how the feasts and festivals established by God in Leviticus 23 point gentiles to the all-inclusive table as well.[1]

Shabbat (v. 3). The first feast mentioned in Leviticus 23 is a weekly sort of feast. It's called the Sabbath or *Shabbat* in Hebrew. A day of rest. The Old Testament is full of instructions, telling and retelling the Israelites to rest from all work on the seventh day of every week, because God created the heavens and the earth in six days and then rested. As Christians, we know that it is only the finished work of Jesus that allows us to experience true rest—both now and forever. God didn't just make the world in six days and then rest; He also made a way back to Himself through Christ so that we might find our ultimate rest in Him.

Passover (v. 5). It was no accident that Jesus's "last supper" with His disciples fell on the Passover. Reclining around the table with His twelve disciples, Jesus gave thanks to the Father, broke the bread, and gave it to His friends.

> "This is my body, which is for you; do this in remembrance of me." In the same way, after supper he took the cup, saying, "This cup is the new covenant in my blood; do this, whenever you drink it, in remembrance of me." (1 Cor. 11:23–25)

To this day, Passover is celebrated not only by Jews but by Messianic Jews and Christians alike because of the beautiful parallels between Jesus and the Passover lamb. Born in a barn and laid in a feeding trough surrounded by shepherds and their sheep, Jesus lived a sinless, unblemished life and was sacrificed as the final and forever Passover lamb. During His last Passover supper, Jesus took His proper place—not *at* the table but *on* it! Jesus didn't come merely to feast with us, He became the feast for us.

What a powerful picture of Jesus, sitting at the table that Passover night, knowing that He, too, would soon be sacrificed. Perhaps He remembered the words his cousin John had spoken when he saw Him walking along the bank of the Jordan River: "Look, the Lamb of God, who takes away the sin of the world!" (John 1:29).

Over 1,500 years before Christ went to the cross, God told His people how to celebrate the Passover. The night before He ushered the Israelites out of captivity in Egypt, He communicated through Moses that each family was to sacrifice a young lamb, then paint the animal's blood over the lintels of their doors. That night, a spirit of death passed through Egypt, killing each firstborn child. But the homes with doorframes covered in the blood of the sacrificed lamb were passed over. Thus, the name Passover. The next day, as the Egyptians were overwhelmed by their grief, the Israelites fled (Exod. 12).

Jesus became the feast for us.

Over the table, Jesus told His friends that another sacrifice was about to take place. When He broke the bread, He explained that He would to be broken too; and when He poured the wine, He let them know that His lifeblood would soon be poured out that our sins might be passed over. Ingesting the words of Christ, His disciples weren't yet able to digest the meaning of Christ until three days later when their teacher returned. Pulling up a chair, He explained it again.

Today it is my hope that you discover what is truly on the table—not just your Bible, but Christ Himself. The Bread of Life was broken for you; the wine that represents His covenant-binding blood was poured out for you. **Christ isn't merely at the table with us now, He's on the table too.**

Feast of Unleavened Bread (v. 6). Immediately after Passover, the Israelites were to spend seven days eating bread made without yeast. God explained this feast before the very first Passover (Exod. 12:17–20), then made it so His people had no choice but to obey (vv. 33–34). After the firstborn sons of Egypt were slain, the Israelites had to leave Egypt quickly. There was no time for the women to add yeast to their dough, so they grabbed it without any yeast and fled.

In the New Testament, Jesus likened yeast to sin when He warned His followers to watch out for the "yeast," or false teaching of the Pharisees and Sadducees (Matt. 16:6). During the original Feast of Unleavened Bread, God warned Israel to leave Egypt's idolatrous sin behind. Today we feast on this same idea: God wants us to be pure and untainted by the world around us. He cleansed us with the blood of Christ and desires for us to remain clean.

Feast of Firstfruits (vv. 9–14). Celebrated on the first Sunday after Passover each year, the Feast of Firstfruits fell symbolically on the first Resurrection Sunday! This celebration was the first of three harvest feasts, and it was a time to give thanks to God for all He provides. As Christians, we know that Christ Himself is the ultimate provision—the firstfruits and the firstborn! The apostle Paul wrote, "But in fact Christ has been raised from the dead, the firstfruits of those who have fallen asleep" (1 Cor. 15:20 ESV). And Scripture states that Jesus was the "firstborn among many brothers and sisters" who would be raised to new life (Rom. 8:29).

Feast of Weeks (vv. 15–21). After the Feast of Firstfruits, the Israelites were to count seven weeks before the Feast of Weeks, or *Shabuot* in Hebrew, which translates to "weeks." This festival was also known as Pentecost because *pentēkonta* means fifty and this harvest celebration takes place fifty days after the first harvest party. During Shabuot the Israelites were to bring two loaves of bread into the temple along with their grain offering. Christians see those two loaves as representing the Jews and the gentiles who came together to form the early church.

On the very first Pentecost after Jesus's resurrection, the Holy Spirit of God fell upon the earliest believers in Christ who were gathered together in Jerusalem. The Holy Spirit enabled them to speak in tongues, languages different from their own. As they spoke truth about God, foreigners who were not from Israel heard their languages being spoken and came to hear (Acts 2:1–12). On that day, three thousand Jews and gentiles put their faith in Jesus as the Messiah (v. 41). Oh, what a picture of the two loaves!

Feast of Trumpets (Lev. 23:23–25). Also known as Rosh Hashanah, the Feast of Trumpets was a celebration of the Jewish New

Year and the third harvest party of the agricultural season. The Israelites would bring God another food offering while blowing on horns and shouting His praise. For us, the Feast of Trumpets points to the day of Christ's return when a trumpet will blast and the Lord will descend (Matt. 24:30–31).

Day of Atonement (vv. 26–32). Ten days after the Feast of Trumpets, on the tenth day of the tenth month was the Day of Atonement, also referred to as Yom Kippur. The Israelites set this day aside to repent of their sin corporately and individually, seeking cleansing and forgiveness. Through the intercession of the high priest, the people were forgiven. Believers in Christ know that Jesus isn't just the Lamb of God, He is also our High Priest: "Therefore, since we have a great high priest who has ascended into heaven, Jesus the Son of God, let us hold firmly to the faith we profess" (Heb. 4:14).

Feast of Tabernacles (vv. 33–36). This seven-day festival, also referred to as Sukkot, allowed the Israelites to creatively celebrate God's provision and protection by building temporary structures and camping outdoors, just as their forefathers did in the wilderness. Today, as Bible-believing Christians, we know that God isn't simply dwelling in His tabernacle; He resides within us. We are His dwelling place (Eph. 2:22).

All the feasts found in the Bible should cause us to feast on the Bible. They are packed with scrumptious symbolism and edible insights! I hope that you enjoyed reading this chapter as much as I enjoyed writing it. As we feast on God's Word, let's remember that Jesus did not come merely to join us at the table; He is the feast on the table as well!

Lamb of God, thank You for giving us so many prophetic and poetic pictures of You through the Old Testament feasts! You gave Your people, Israel, regulations for feasting because You wanted to feast with them regularly, and You want to fellowship with me regularly at the table as well. I'm catching the vision and getting hungry for You, the ultimate feast. In the name of the Passover lamb, Jesus, Amen.

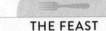

THE FEAST

Leviticus 23

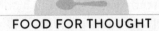

FOOD FOR THOUGHT

Based on what you read in Leviticus 23, consider these questions:

- What did I learn about God?
- What did I learn about myself?
- How do I need to live differently as a result?

day 35

FOR ONE AND ALL

For whatever was written in former days was written for our instruction, that through endurance and through the encouragement of the Scriptures we might have hope.

Romans 15:4 ESV

IN 1536 BIBLICAL SCHOLAR AND LINGUIST William Tyndale was strangled and then burned at the stake in Antwerp, Belgium. The charge against him was heresy. His crime? Translating the Bible from Hebrew and Greek into English.[1] At the time, the Roman Catholic Church throughout the world read the Scriptures in Latin alone, and in England, it was a crime punishable by death to translate them into English.

When both the church and the king forbade Tyndale's translation project in 1523, the zealous young reformer fled to Germany, where he completed the English version of the New Testament. Once printed, it was smuggled back into his homeland in 1525. He was still abroad and working on translating the Old Testament when he was captured and later martyred for his service to God and his fellow man.

As an Oxford educated scholar who was fluent in Latin, Greek, and Hebrew, Tyndale was one of a small number of Englishmen able to read and understand the Scriptures in their original languages. Not only did he read God's Word, he believed it with all his heart. William could never remain content hoarding away the Scriptures as his own private possession. Once Tyndale had read and received the good news for himself, he had to share it with others, regardless of the danger.

Foxe's Book of Martyrs, first published in 1563, features this recounting of an exchange between Tyndale and another learned man who challenged him.

> The [learned man] burst out into these blasphemous words, "We were better to be without God's laws than the pope's." Master Tyndale, hearing this, full of godly zeal, and not bearing that blasphemous saying, replied, "I defy the pope, and all his laws" and added, "If God spared [my] life, ere many years [I] would cause a boy that driveth the plough to know more of the Scripture than [the pope] did."[2]

I can only imagine what Tyndale must have thought when he translated these words written by the apostle Paul: "For whatever was written in former days was written for our instruction, that through endurance and through the encouragement of the Scriptures we might have hope" (Rom. 15:4 ESV). Tyndale longed to share the simple, applicable, and life-giving hope that God so generously offered all of humanity through His Word.

He was not opposed to the church or the government but to anyone who kept the gospel of Jesus Christ from the common people. That was the sole reason Tyndale defied both king and clergy: "For if God be on our side, what matter maketh it who be against us, be they bishops, cardinals, popes, or whatsoever names they will?"[3] With single-minded devotion, he risked his life to see the Holy Scriptures readable and holdable, available and consumable, for one and all.

At the time of his death, with eighteen thousand copies of the New Testament secretly in circulation,[4] Tyndale said, "I call God to record against the day we shall appear before our Lord Jesus, that I never altered one syllable of God's Word against my conscience, nor would do this day if all that is in earth, whether it be honor, pleasure, or riches, might be given me."[5]

During the Protestant Reformation in Europe, between 1500 and 1558, over six hundred men and women were burned at the stake for their bold faith in Christ and their firm conviction that all people must have direct access to God Himself, through the encouragement of the Scriptures.[6]

Seventy-five years after William Tyndale's death, in 1611, King James I of England finally allowed the printing and distribution of the Bible in English. Today we refer to this early translation as the King James Bible. Since that time, the Bible (whether in whole or in part) has been translated into thousands of languages.

The Bible is now readily available to us, but we are not as available to it as we ought to be.

With the Bible so widely available, it's hard not to wonder why so many Bible-believing Christians are still not Bible-reading Christians. Perhaps it's because we've developed a "been there, done that" mentality. The Bible is now readily available to us, but we are not as available to it as we ought to be.

When author and pastor Eugene Peterson was asked why he wrote The Message, a reading Bible translated into conversational English, he responded:

While I was teaching a class on Galatians, I began to realize that the adults in my class weren't feeling the vitality and directness that I sensed as I read and studied the New Testament in its original Greek. Writing straight from the original text, I began to attempt to bring into English the rhythms and idioms of the original language. I knew that the early readers of the New Testament were captured and engaged by these writings and I wanted my congregation to be impacted in the same way. . . . I hoped to bring the New Testament to life for two different types of people: those who hadn't read the Bible because it seemed too distant and irrelevant and those who had read the Bible so much that it had become "old hat."[7]

Whether you are new to Bible reading or have read it so much it's become old hat, I hope that today's reading reminds you how privileged we are to have God's written Word available to us. For though it was written long ago, it "was written for our instruction, that through endurance and through the encouragement of the Scriptures we might have hope" (Rom. 15:4 ESV).

Peterson's Spirit-filled interpretation says it this way:

Even if it was written in Scripture long ago, you can be sure it's written for *us*. God wants the combination of his steady, constant calling and warm, personal counsel in Scripture to come to characterize *us*, keeping us alert for whatever he will do next. May our dependably steady and warmly personal God develop maturity in you so that you get along with each other as well as Jesus gets along with us all. Then we'll be a choir—not our voices only, but our very lives singing in harmony in a stunning anthem to the God and Father of our Master Jesus! (Rom. 15:4–6)

Though written long ago, the Bible was written for each and every one of us today!

Lord, thank You for making Your Word available to me. Help me to press on and persevere in reading the Scriptures. Help me to glean instruction and encouragement from them. And then, Lord, help me to share Your Word with those who don't yet have it. In the generous, Bible-breathing name of Jesus, Amen.

THE FEAST

Romans 15

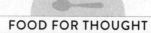

FOOD FOR THOUGHT

After reading Romans 15, answer the following questions:

- What did I learn about God?
- What did I learn about myself?
- How do I need to live differently as a result?

The task of Bible translation is not yet complete!

I mentioned on day 7 that one of my favorite ministries to partner with in the ongoing work of Bible translation and distribution is The Seed Company. Working with local translators and missionaries throughout the world, The Seed Company comes alongside them with training and publishing support to help make William Tyndale's dream a reality for all!

It is my joy to invite you to join our feasting community in actively supporting the ongoing work of Bible translation today. Prayerfully consider partnering with The Seed Company as they bring the good news of Jesus Christ to the far reaches of our world. Find out more at www.seedcompany .com.

day 36

WHEN PROGRESSIVE
IS REGRESSIVE

> Woe to those who call evil good
>   and good evil,
> who put darkness for light
>   and light for darkness,
> who put bitter for sweet
>   and sweet for bitter!
>
> Isaiah 5:20 ESV

DID YOU KNOW that it's possible to edit an article on Wikipedia? I discovered this when one of my teenage sons jokingly made a few edits to a random page. After a few laughs and a little parenting on my part, he changed it back. No harm done—in this case. It turns out that anyone with an internet connection can change things around. Some pages have gatekeepers who monitor and correct inaccurate edits, but the fact of the matter is we're living in an era that considers truth relative and definitions fluid. Even issues once considered black-and-white are now seen as gray.

At the top of each Wikipedia page is a tab that invites readers to "edit" its content. The moment I tapped that link, this pop-up message appeared: "Anyone can edit, and every improvement helps. Thank you for helping the world discover more."

My stomach lurched as I read that message the first time. Though it sounds affirming, it's actually disturbing, because not all "corrections" are correct. Changing a definition has the power to change people's thinking and ultimately their living. While some believe this sort of open-mindedness is progressive, not all steps forward move us closer to truth. Today truth is relative and open for interpretation, and that is dangerous. "Every improvement helps" is not always true. Some edits hinder and hurt. Some edits are unholy, especially when they lead us to call evil good and good evil.

Truth is being "deconstructed." Truth with a capital *T* is being edited with a lowercase *T* to include one and all. It's being taken apart, broken down, rewritten, and reevaluated through the lens of any given individual's life experiences, opinions, wounds, and wants. And this isn't just happening on Wikipedia; it's also present within the church. In many Christian circles, deconstruction is considered "progressive." It's seen as moving us forward in the areas of authenticity and inclusivity. However, this movement, labeled "progressive Christianity," threatens regression, backing us out of biblical truth altogether and into the current of cultural edits.

Deconstruction works like a bulldozer, knocking down historical Christianity. Then it invites churches and churchgoers to reconstruct a more palatable version of our faith. Unfortunately, clearing the ground will eventually leave us with no solid ground on which to stand—unless we hold firm the unchanging Word of God. But the only way to do that is to know God's Word and hold it as our standard for truth.

Do you see why these forty days of feasting are so important? This isn't about developing a sweet tooth for some feel-good Bible experience. We must learn to regularly ingest God's authoritative Word for ourselves if we are to know what is true and what is not, especially when the cultural sands shift beneath our feet. Without that biblical bedrock, we'll find ourselves slipping on the edits that slip into our local churches and Christian communities.

We must be on guard, my Bible-believing friends, because progressive Christianity identifies itself as real Christianity, but it is not. Progressive Christianity does not attempt to understand the world based on what the Bible says but looks to understand the Bible based on what the world and our emotions tell us is true. This is why we must actively study the Word for ourselves. The more we understand what God says, the more prepared we'll be when our emotions or those around us attempt to edit God's Truth to align with their "truth."

Minister E. Paul Hovey once said that people "do not reject the Bible because it contradicts itself but because it contradicts them."[1] Goodness, isn't that the era in which we find ourselves today? We are so offended by biblical truth that contradicts culture that we're willing to edit what the Bible says to better accommodate our cultural values. This is why we must cling to the truth of the unchanging Scriptures. We must not reject God's Word, even if it hurts our feelings and contradicts our desires. We don't get to pick and choose what's comfortable and leave out anything that makes us uncomfortable.

In the aftermath of deconstructing one's faith, what is typically rebuilt is not the gospel of Jesus Christ, but a self-made gospel suited to each person's preference. In her book *Another Gospel?*, author Alisa Childers wrote,

> In the context of faith, deconstruction is the process of systematically dissecting and often rejecting the beliefs you grew up with. Sometimes the Christian will deconstruct all the way into atheism. Some remain there, but others experience reconstruction. But the type of faith they end up embracing almost never resembles the Christianity they formerly knew. . . .
>
> Progressive Christianity is not simply a shift in the Christian view of social issues. . . . It's an entirely different religion—with another Jesus—and another gospel.[2]

This is a warning bell for us to wake up and actively guard our hearts and minds with biblical truth. If we want to progress in our faith, moving forward in Christlikeness, we cannot progress beyond Christ. For many people today, moving forward in their biblical worldview actually moves them out of the Bible entirely and into the world. That's not for us. We must not edit truth to align with our lives, but rather edit our lives to align with the Truth. And the only way to edit our lives is to lay them down on the altar of God's transforming Word. **The Bible was given to change us, not the other way around.** God knows we're the ones in need of a holy edit.

So how do we guard ourselves against the pull of progressive Christian culture? While it's good to be aware of false narratives, false teachers, and false doctrine, it's better to focus on what's true.

I've heard it said that when a person is hired to work in the counterfeit department of the US Treasury they are given a stack of currency to study. However, the bills they receive are not what you might expect. Instead of being handed counterfeit bills, they are given the real deal. The idea is that when someone who knows what is true comes across something false, they will know it because they are so familiar with what the real deal looks like, feels like, and sounds like. We must be seekers of truth in a world full of frauds. The apostle Paul put it this way:

We must be seekers of truth in a world full of frauds.

> For the time will come when people will not tolerate sound doctrine *and* accurate instruction [that challenges them with God's truth]; but *wanting* to have their ears tickled [with something pleasing], they will accumulate for themselves [many] teachers [one after another, chosen] to satisfy their own desires *and* to support the errors they hold. (2 Tim. 4:3 AMP)

We live in an era when good is called evil and evil is called good, light is considered dark and dark is considered light, and bitter tastes sweet and what was once savored as sweet now bursts with bitterness (Isa. 5:20). That's why we're looking at the basic tenets of progressive Christianity. As we hold them up to the lamplight of God's unchanging Word, we will discover that this new gospel is not the gospel at all.

The progressive gospel is not centered around the atoning cross of Christ but merely aims for Christlikeness. However, Jesus didn't come to set a good example, He came to set us free. Jesus set us free from our bondage to sin, and He used the cross to do it. He is more than a role model, He is the Way, the Truth, and the Life that ushers us into a forever life with the Father (John 14:6). Yes, we want to walk as He walked and live as He lived and treat others the way He would treat them, but that all requires the cross of Christ.

Progressive Christians focus on moralism and good works, especially regarding issues of social justice. Bible-believing Christians are well aware that they are sinners saved by grace alone. It is only because they have been made right that they are able to live right, with the ongoing help of the Holy Spirit. Being a good person is impossible without the redemptive work of Jesus. We must cling to the cross that many are attempting to edit away.

Progressive Christians don't just downplay sin, they take offense when Christ followers suggest that sin separates humanity from God. While they sincerely believe they are being kind, eternally speaking, this is the unkindest thing a person can do. To disregard sin is to reject the reality of our separation from a holy God. When we do that, we no longer need a savior. As a result, sinners remain in their sin, separated forever, never knowing the love of a redeeming God.

When we deny the presence of sin, the gospel ceases to be good news. But when we believe the truth of the old adage that God hates the sin but loves the sinner, we see that the most loving thing of all is to hold firm to a biblical view of sin, that we might share salvation with those still stuck in sin's shackles.

Brothers and sisters, we simply have to know the truth of God's Word so we can recognize falsehood when we encounter it. Though culture tells us that it's hateful to confront sin, God tells us clearly that every single one of us "have sinned and fall short of the glory of God" (Rom. 3:23). There's no mistaking the consequences we deserve, "for the wages of sin is death, but the gift of God is eternal life in Christ Jesus our Lord" (Rom. 6:23). That's right! "God demonstrates his own love for us in this: While we were still sinners, Christ died for us" (Rom. 5:8). As Bible-believing people, we know that if we confess with our lips that "'Jesus is Lord,' and believe in [our hearts] that God raised him from the dead, [we] will be saved" (Rom. 10:9–10). There is no other name under heaven by which we can be saved (Acts 4:12). Only Jesus.

The progressive movement of today invites everyone to come as they are, while refusing to address what they are: sinners in need of grace. The invitation must remain, "Come as you are," but through the reading and loving application of God's Word—praise Him—we don't have to remain as we are! This is the good news of the gospel. Let's not let the world edit away that loving truth!

Lord, help me to progress only down the road of biblical truth. Help me stand firm against falsehood and unbiblical edits. In the name of Jesus, the Truth, Amen.

THE FEAST

2 Timothy 4

FOOD FOR THOUGHT

There are two profound things to notice in 2 Timothy 4. First, note the hardships Paul endured because of the truth that he shared. Then notice his friendships. Many of his closest friends deserted him when things got tough. How about you? Are you ready to stand firm on the unchanging Word of God, even if everyone else goes the way of the world? As we near the end of our forty-day feast, I am asking myself the same question.

day 37

TEST AND SEE

Beware of false prophets, who come to you in sheep's clothing but inwardly are ravenous wolves.

Matthew 7:15 ESV

YESTERDAY we considered some of the false teachings that have filtered into many churches today. I encouraged you to know what is biblically true (Truth with a capital *T*) in order to recognize teaching about the Bible that is untrue. While one of the main themes of our feast is "taste and see," we also need to "test and see" if what some teach as God's Word is actually consistent with the whole of Scripture.

In Matthew 7:15 Jesus cautioned us about false prophets, and Paul warned the early church leaders not to allow *themselves* to slip into false teaching when he said,

Keep watch over yourselves and all the flock of which the Holy Spirit has made you overseers. Be shepherds of the church of God, which he bought with his own blood. I know that after I leave, savage wolves will come in among you and will not spare the flock. Even from your own number men will arise and distort the truth in order to draw away disciples after them. So be on your guard! Remember that for three years I never stopped warning each of you night and day with tears. (Acts 20:28–31)

Other warnings date back to the Old Testament. Here's what God spoke through Jeremiah: "The prophets are prophesying lies in my name. I have not sent them or appointed them or spoken to them. They are prophesying to you false visions, divinations, idolatries and the delusions of their own minds" (14:14).

Testing the teaching of our teachers against the inerrant whole of Scripture is essential. I am not suggesting that we think of ourselves more highly than we ought, or that we sit under the authority of our pastors with judgmental and distrusting spirits. But we must know what God has said so that we can know when others contradict Him.

This is not limited to the pastors and Bible teachers within our brick-and-mortar churches. Today we have more online "Christian influencers" influencing us than ever before. I am one of them, as I post daily Bible verses, quotes, and prayers, and teach from the Scriptures in books such as this one.

The apostle Paul's warning in Acts 20 is sobering, to be sure, but it is James's words to teachers that cause me to tremble as I post Bible verses online, speak to women's groups throughout the country, and teach the Bible within the pages of books: "Not many of you should become teachers, my fellow believers, because you know that we who teach will be judged more strictly" (3:1).

That warning is for me, but this warning is for you: you must know enough of what God has said about Himself in order to discern if what others have to say about Him is true. The complicating part is that much of God's instructions don't feel good, so when we get those feel-good, affirming messages from our teachers, we tend to like them more. But 2 Timothy 4:3–4 gives us a clear warning:

The time will come when people will not put up with sound doctrine. Instead, to suit their own desires, they will gather around them a great number of teachers to say what their itching ears want to hear. They will turn their ears away from the truth and turn aside to myths.

I've heard it said that sometimes "the truth hurts," but God is kind and promises that the Truth ultimately sets us free. As Bible-believing Christians, we must know and ultimately guard the truth or there will be no truth left in our hearts, in our homes, or in our churches. If we don't cling to truth, it will morph subtly into something entirely different. And subtly is often how it goes. I'm reminded of the way the serpent in the garden—the deceiving devil himself—didn't outright tell Eve to disobey. Instead, he casually questioned, "Did God really say, 'You must not eat from any tree in the garden?'" (Gen. 3:1). Though Eve clarified that it was only that one tree they had been forbidden to feast on, the sly serpent planted a seed of doubt that caused her to question God's clear command: "Don't eat from that tree or you will surely die" (Gen. 2:17, author's paraphrase).

Oh my, don't we hear the same conversation happening in our world and even in our churches today? "Did God really say . . . ?" **Redefining words may be what ultimately defines this generation.** If we're not careful, we will redefine God's truth until we have redefined our way out of truth altogether. Which is why Jesus's warning in Mathew 7 is for us today. Good and godly men and women are being led astray and encouraged to question what God really said in His Word.

First Kings 13 tells the story of such a man, a prophet who was good, godly, and well intentioned. The Bible does not name him but calls him a "man of God" (v. 1). He was sent by God with a message for Jeroboam, the king of Israel, in Bethel. As King Jeroboam made unholy sacrifices and did all sorts of evil, the man of God cried out against the altar. When the evil king extended his hand against God's prophet, yelling "Seize him!" Jeroboam's hand shriveled up (v. 4).

King Jeroboam begged the man of God to heal his crippled hand. So the holy man prayed to God on the king's behalf, and

Jeroboam's hand was healed. With a mixture of sincere gratitude and healthy fear, the king invited the prophet back to his palace to dine with him and receive both his thanks and a reward. But the godly man replied,

> "If you give me half your house, I will not go in with you. And I will not eat bread or drink water in this place, for so was it commanded me by the word of the LORD, saying, 'You shall neither eat bread nor drink water nor return by the way that you came.'" So he went another way and did not return by the way that he came to Bethel." (vv. 8–10 ESV)

So far, so good, right? But the story didn't end there. Unfortunately for the man of God, there was another prophet who lived in Bethel. He was an old man whose sons told him everything that had happened. The old prophet responded by telling his sons to saddle his donkey, then he went out after the man of God. Finding him under an oak tree, the old prophet said, "Come home with me and eat bread" (vv. 11–15 ESV).

But the man of God replied, "I may not return with you, or go in with you, neither will I eat bread nor drink water with you in this place, for it was said to me by the word of the LORD, 'You shall neither eat bread nor drink water there, nor return by the way that you came'" (vv. 16–17 ESV).

We must know what God has told us to do and not do.

Then the old prophet told a bald-faced lie, declaring, "I also am a prophet as you are, and an angel spoke to me by the word of the LORD, saying, 'Bring him back with you into your house that he may eat bread and drink water.'" (v. 18 ESV). In clear disobedience to God's command, the man of God broke bread with the deceiver, and in the end he died (v. 24).

This story is a clear call for church leaders and churchgoers, for shepherds and their sheep. Let us not be led astray. We must know what God has told us to do and not do, and we must not believe others when they tell us that we misunderstood divine directives.

Rarely does the devil tell us to outright disobey and disregard God's commands; instead, he invites us to reconsider and redefine them. He is a wolf in sheep's clothing and has walked right past many shepherds and into our folds. This is why we need to be biblically literate and steadfast in holding to the truth when others tempt us with lies that are more comfortable.

This is difficult to teach and difficult to learn. Let us pray to the Spirit to help us.

Spirit of Truth, teach me to know truth, cling to truth, and obey truth. I don't want to redefine Your Word or sit under the teaching of those who do. Give me a discerning spirit and a steadfast understanding of Your holy commands. And, as always, help me to obey. I ask all of this in the name of Jesus, Amen.

THE FEAST

1 Kings 13

FOOD FOR THOUGHT

Based on what you read in 1 Kings 13, consider these questions:

- What did I learn about God?
- What did I learn about myself?
- How do I need to live differently as a result?

day 38

FINISHING STRONG

My soul is weary with sorrow;
strengthen me according to your word.

Psalm 119:28

IN THE MONTHS that I was writing this book, my family and I experienced enough personal challenges to fill a book of its own. As we struggled through one traumatic episode after another, I often closed my laptop, but I never closed my Bible. There were times I stopped writing, but I didn't stop reading. If anything, I feasted more on God's promises than I had in a very long time. Occasionally I had to let go of *this* book to cling tight to the Good Book!

During that season, these words from the psalmist jumped off the page of my Bible in a very personal way: "My soul is weary with sorrow; strengthen me according to your word" (Ps. 119:28). It became my prayer, and I'm happy to say it is now an answered prayer. Though many of our challenges are still challenging, the Lord has given me His strength, and I am ready to wrap up our feast with some encouragement for those who are weary.

God uses His Word to strengthen us when we are weak. God feeds us joy when we are joyless, for His Word is sweet when life is bitter. He serves us faith when we are faithless and hope when we are hopeless. He spoon-feeds us courage when we ache down deep from fear. Our Bibles make us brave to continue when we are tempted to quit.

How kind of the Lord to use that hard season in order to bring a sweet ending to this feast. Amid my own pain, God gave me greater compassion for those who are in pain. In my own tender weariness, I am tenderhearted toward those who are weary with sorrow and weak beyond measure. I pray that today's chapter encourages you in a deeply meaningful way. I would not have been able to meet you in your suffering had I not experienced my own. And so it is with a recently revived heart that I invite us both back to the table today.

Over the course of that difficult season, I learned firsthand how spiritual food truly is the sustenance we need to endure. We know that if we were to stop eating literal food, most of us would die within a couple of weeks. Our internal organs would slow down and eventually shut down. Our physical beings are dependent on food. Nutrients bring life to our bodies. Carbohydrates break down and turn into energy while protein builds muscle. We need food, no doubt, but now we know that this is just a metaphor for the feast we need most.

We need a steady diet of God's Word to remain steady in this life; we need His Word to provide us with the muscular strength to persevere. God's Word gives us the energy to lift our hands in praise and lift our eyes to the mountains, to look up to the Lord, our true source of strength (Ps. 121:1–2). We need His Word to speak to our hearts so that we might experience His sweetness, especially when our circumstances do not taste sweet. His Word offers comfort and compassion to those in desperate need. And through His promises, hope is promised to the hopeless, love is extended to the unlovely, and joy is proclaimed!

At the birth of our sweet Savior, an angel announced His coming to a group of shepherds—considered the lowliest of all humans at that time—who were keeping watch over their flocks by night. "And the angel said to them, 'Fear not, for behold, I bring you good news of great joy that will be for all the people'" (Luke 2:10 ESV).

That's what God's Word is—good news of great joy for all people!

Because this painful season in our family life coincided with the Christmas season, the angel's proclamation, promising *me* great joy, ministered to my heart as I struggled with a lack of joy. Other themes within the nativity narrative ministered to me as well. Perhaps the most energy-enabling, strength-sustaining, perseverance-providing verse was Matthew 1:23: "'The virgin will conceive and give birth to a son, and they will call him Immanuel' (which means 'God with us')." More than anything, I needed to know that God was with me.

Maybe that's the Bible promise you need to ingest today. God is near. Though you may be going through difficult circumstances, His promise to never leave your side is certain and secure. "Be strong and courageous. Do not be afraid or terrified because of them, for the LORD your God goes with you; he will never leave you nor forsake you" (Deut. 31:6).

I don't know who "them" refers to in the context of your life right now, but when enemies advance into your camp, whether in the form of circumstances, people, or the devil himself, remember this promise penned by the psalmist: "You prepare a table before me in the presence of my enemies" (Ps. 23:5). What a beautiful picture of God's constant wooing and clear invitation back to the table, even during our fiercest battles. **When our enemies are pressing hard against us, we must press into our closest ally.**

God's Word brings sweetness to our lives, even in the bitterest of seasons.

Though it sometimes feels like we are on the brink of death, His Word is alive and gives life to our bones. Each Bible passage has the power to transcend its historical context and apply directly to the context of our daily struggles. This good news is not reserved for the Israelites and ancient times alone but affords us "great joy" today. God's Word brings sweetness to our lives, even in the bitterest of seasons.

On day 7 of our feast, I shared John 1:14 with you: "The Word became flesh and made his dwelling among us." Perhaps you recall that the meaning of the Greek word *logos*, which is usually translated "word," can be more fully understood as "complete message." God the Father sent the complete message of His redeeming love by wrapping His message in flesh and sending it to us in the form of a Messenger, His Son. The birth of the Messenger was the birth of the Word made flesh—Emmanuel, God with us!

Jesus was born in a stable with shepherds all around. There were likely sheep in their midst, possibly trying to nibble hay from the manger. Jesus was the ultimate Passover lamb. The feast in a feeding trough. I guess we could say that God put the "table" in "*stable*," then invited us to pull up a chair.

Jesus has been our feast for the last thirty-eight days. I hope that you have savored and seen, tasted and tested, discovered and delighted in how good He is!

Messiah, Jesus, Lamb of God, Emmanuel, God with us, thank You for coming into the world and into my life. I have tasted and seen and concluded that nothing and no one but You can ever satisfy me. In all Your names, I joyfully pray, Amen.

THE FEAST

Luke 2

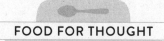

FOOD FOR THOUGHT

Though I have always known God's Word is good, it became even better to me, sweeter and more sustaining, during our family's difficult season. Whether you are in a difficult season or the most joyous one you've ever known, take a moment to reflect on the angel's promise in Luke 2:10, that the coming of Jesus into our lives brings great joy. Feast on that!

day 39

GONE FISHIN'

Therefore go and make disciples of all nations, baptizing them
in the name of the Father and of the Son and of the Holy Spirit.

Matthew 28:19

MY GOAL IN WRITING THIS BOOK wasn't to serve up forty
days of meals to keep Jesus-hungry men and women dependent
on more supplementary Bible resources. The goal was never to
feed you, but to inspire and equip you to feed yourself. Perhaps
you've heard the old adage, "Give a man a fish and you feed him
for a day. Teach a man to fish and you feed him for a lifetime."
**This book was never intended to be a forty-day feast that comes
to an end, but a gateway into a feasting life that never ends.** It
is my hope that you not only develop an appetite for God's Word
but also the confidence to open it up and consume it on your own.

Think of this book as a metaphorical lunch basket containing a few fish and loaves. When Jesus's disciples presented Him
with such a meal, He multiplied their meager offering and fed five
thousand men, along with all the women and children who had
come out to the mountainside to hear Him teach. This forty-day

feast is my small offering. It's not enough to get you through your life, but God can multiply what you've learned here as you pick up your figurative fishing net and cast it over the waters of His Word each day.

My ultimate desire is that the meal lasts even longer than your own lifetime of feasting. It's my sincere hope that as you learn to fish in the deep waters of God's Word, you will hear Jesus's call to feed others who are hungry and then teach them to feed themselves. Jesus never called us to be solitary fishers; He always intended us to be fishers of people.

The more confident you become reading and applying God's Word to your life, the greater your hunger will become to share the feast with others. Well-fed Christians must come to a point where it feels gluttonous to keep the feast to themselves when so many around the world (and around their block) are starving. At the start of these forty days I stated that most Bible-believing men and women are not Bible-reading men and women. Now that you are, take your Bible reading one step further: Bible believers who are Bible readers eventually become Bible teachers!

> *God invited simple men and women to simply follow Him.*

Perhaps you'll begin by simply sharing a Bible verse on social media or texting it to a friend. In time, becoming a fisher of people might look like a neighborhood Bible study around your kitchen table, where all good feasts are served.

I understand that there are many different personality types. Some people love to host and feel comfortable inviting others into their home, regardless of how big, small, picked up, or messy it is. Others can't imagine speaking in front of a few friends, let alone praying out loud. That's why it's important to remember that Jesus didn't call skilled orators to follow Him; he called ordinary men and women, like a tax collector, a fisherman, and a handful of others.

God invited simple men and women to simply follow Him, and He extends the same invitation to us today. When we say yes to following Jesus, however, a time must come when we invite others to follow us as we follow Him. Don't wait until you are a perfect, glowing example of a Christ follower. Extend the invitation as you stumble along the road, fishing pole in hand, pointing others toward the water and the One who walked upon it.

Even when the apostle Paul admitted his limitations, he didn't let them keep him from inviting others to join him:

> Not that I have already obtained all this, or have already arrived at my goal, but I press on to take hold of that for which Christ Jesus took hold of me. Brothers and sisters, I do not consider myself yet to have taken hold of it. But one thing I do: Forgetting what is behind and straining toward what is ahead, I press on toward the goal to win the prize for which God has called me heavenward in Christ Jesus. . . . *Join together in following my example, brothers and sisters.* (Phil. 3:12–14, 17, emphasis added)

Drop anchor and cast your line in the deep waters of Scripture, but remember that learning to fish should never be for your benefit alone. Share what you catch with others, then teach others to fish for themselves.

While Jesus's first words to some of his disciples were, "Follow me," His last words to them all, before ascending into heaven, are known as the Great Commission. Jesus gave His disciples this charge: "Therefore go and make disciples of all nations, baptizing them in the name of the Father and of the Son and of the Holy Spirit" (Matt. 28:19). First, He invited them with a command to follow. Then He charged them to extend that invitation to others. The more time you spend in your Bible, the more the Great Commission will become your mission.

Those who first received the Great Commission saw Jesus's miracles firsthand. They walked with Him, listened to Him, and witnessed His authority over sin and death. It's as though He was saying to His closest companions, "*Therefore*, since I have revealed Myself to you, reveal Me to others. Now, go!"

The disciples ate with Jesus for just three years during His earthly ministry, but once He left them, they devoted the rest of their ministering lives to sharing Him with a starving world. Likewise, when we feast with Jesus at the table of His Word, we've got to start pulling up chairs and inviting others to join us. Once you learn to feast, it is time to share your food.

Jesus's first disciples were fishermen. Fishing was their job, but Jesus called them to become fishers of men. Jesus turned their profession into a profession of faith. Today their job becomes ours. We are to be fishers of men and women, boys and girls. No matter what our job is, our profession of faith is the number one call on our lives once we put our faith in Christ.

The apostle Paul urged those in the church in Rome to share their faith, writing,

How then will they call on him in whom they have not believed? And how are they to believe in him of whom they have never heard? And how are they to hear without someone preaching? And how are they to preach unless they are sent? As it is written, "How beautiful are the feet of those who preach the good news!" (10:14–15 ESV)

How beautiful are the Jesus-hungry men and women who have learned to cast their nets into the deep waters of God's Word and now share their catch with others.

Today, as you feast on Jesus's first and last invitations, I pray that you catch more than fish. The goal is that you catch a vision of how you might invite others to feast on God's Word with you!

Lord, I am learning to fish and finding Your Word deeply filling. Thank You. But the next step is outside my comfort zone. Give me courage and give me vision. Show me what it looks like to be a fisher of Your people. I'm willing to invite others to pull up a chair and start feasting on Your Word with me, and I'm listening as I ask all this in Jesus's name, Amen.

THE FEAST

Matthew 4:18–22
Matthew 14:13–21
Matthew 28:16–20

FOOD FOR THOUGHT

Based on what you read in today's passages, consider these questions:

- What did I learn about God?
- What did I learn about myself?
- How do I need to live differently as a result?

Once you've answered those questions, jot down the names of some of your friends and family members, your neighbors or coworkers, who God might want you to extend this invitation to: "Let's follow Jesus together!"

day 40

SEVEN MORE DAYS!

The Israelites who were present in Jerusalem celebrated the Festival of Unleavened Bread for seven days with great rejoicing, while the Levites and priests praised the LORD every day with resounding instruments dedicated to the LORD. . . .

The whole assembly then agreed to celebrate the festival seven more days; so for another seven days they celebrated joyfully.

2 Chronicles 30:21, 23

AWESTRUCK AND INSPIRED, I pushed myself back from the desk where my Bible sat open, stood to my feet, and clapped my hands in delight. I had just read the passage above from 2 Chronicles 30. At the time, I was only beginning to outline this forty-day devotional, but as soon as my eyes consumed that passage, I knew I'd found the sweet dessert I would serve at the end of our feast! But before we get ahead of ourselves and apply this passage to the context of our feasting days, let's take a moment to understand the story in its biblical context.

Hezekiah, the king of Judah at that time, had just ascended to the throne. He was only twenty-five years old, but he leapt into action. Within the very first year of his reign, Hezekiah reestablished temple worship and animal sacrifices because his father, King Ahaz, had ignored the Lord's commands completely and led the nation into blatant idolatry. God's house had fallen apart, and His people had fallen away. King Hezekiah, however, was adamant that the people of Judah needed to be cleansed from their collective sins and return to the Lord immediately, so he charged the Levites to consecrate themselves, the temple, and all the utensils for service. Then he sent an invitation throughout the kingdom, imploring the people to return to the God of their ancestors and come to Jerusalem to celebrate the Passover feast. And they came.

After the Passover, the party rolled into the seven-day Feast of Unleavened Bread. Consuming all that unraised bread, it seems, worked to raise their faith, and raise their spirits, until they raised their trumpets and their voices in praise, shouting, "Seven more days! Let's celebrate for seven more days!"

Returning to the Lord's temple brought them back to His table. After years of idolatry and the painful consequences of sin, God's people experienced joy in His presence, and they didn't want it to end. This is exactly where I hope you find yourself today—seated at the Lord's right hand, experiencing the fullness of His joy and an abundance of good things, satisfied yet salivating.

Just as the Judeans celebrated their return to the Lord's temple, praising Him for the generous way He received them back at the table, we should be making some noise, begging for more feasting days as well! We've tasted and seen how good God's presence is, how fulfilling His Word is, and now we find ourselves hungrier than ever before, not wanting the feast to end.

"Can we keep going?"

It's that very desire to keep going that led me to write this book in the first place. Every January, I lead a 40-Day Sugar Fast online. Each time that I do, thousands of men and women are convicted that they have been turning to sweet treats to get them through their days for far too long. Instead of running to Christ to get them through their struggles and sadness, loneliness and lethargy, they run to lattes and brownies. Rather than feasting on God's Word to meet their needs, they consume other things—but God never intended those things to get us through our hardest days. Over time, false fillers become false gods. When we don't turn to Christ as our stronghold, the things we do turn to for saving can become a different sort of stronghold, holding us back from experiencing Christ's strong hold. This is why we fast: We set down those temporary, feel-good pleasures in order to taste and see how good and sweet God is. **We fast in order to feast.**

Over time, false fillers become false gods.

At the end of that forty-day fast each year, the requests start rolling in: "Can we keep going?" "Do we have to stop?" At first I thought those making the requests were asking to keep fasting, but it finally dawned on me that what they really wanted was to keep feasting! They desired more servings from God's Word. This book was my response. My goal, however, was not to feed my Jesus-hungry friends for another forty days, but to inspire and equip them to feed themselves for a lifetime.

We need to be fed daily, not weekly and not merely on Sunday mornings with a pastor serving up sermons. Your pastor never intended for you to stay satiated all week long because of something they cooked up and served at the start of the week. No! Each Sunday feast should leave us shouting, "Seven days! We need seven days of feasting!" I don't know a single pastor who isn't hungry for that response.

In Acts we read that the early church "received the word with all eagerness, examining the Scriptures *daily*" (17:11 ESV, emphasis added). Are you eagerly opening and examining the Scriptures daily now? Do you come to your Bible hungrily anticipating the way it will encourage your heart, refresh your spirit, and restore your faith? And are you feeling more equipped and less intimidated by the veritable smorgasbord of chapters and verses, stories and songs, histories and prophecies? You've tasted and seen how they all point to the One who is our feast: the Word made flesh, the Lamb of God, the Bread of Life, and the Living Water—Jesus Himself! He's who we're most hungry for, and now we know where to find Him.

Jesus is at the table, and He's on the table. What's more, He placed a sweeping banner proclaiming "love" over our banqueting table (see Song of Songs 2:4). Yes! His Word is His love letter. His story is the history of His loving pursuit. Jesus came to chase us down in our waywardness and bring us back into a right and restored relationship with the Father. Your Bible, there on the table, is your invitation.

There is no way to write "The End" here as we wrap up this forty-day feast, for this is the beginning. Now is the time for you to make the radical choice to keep going. If you have not yet started a Bible reading plan, it's time to make one. Begin at the beginning, in Genesis. Or start in Matthew and read through the Gospels, then keep on reading. Roll right into the book of Acts, then into the letters sent to the early church. Those letters were written for you, for you are the church of God today. The whole Bible was written for you and sent to you, a letter to His beloved.

Remember to read the Word slowly, savoring it as you go. Bring along a commentary as your guide when things get confusing, but don't forget the ultimate Guide, the Holy Spirit. As you open your Bible, open your heart to Him and humbly confess, "I'm ready to hear from You today." Then, as you read, prayerfully consider these three questions:

- What did I learn about God?
- What did I learn about myself?
- How do I apply it to my life in a way that leaves me looking more like Jesus?

Don't rush this meal by gulping it down in one bite and then moving on unchanged. Ingest it, then carefully digest it. **Savor the flavor of God's Word, then let its sweetness permeate your life.**

It has been my great joy to invite you to the table these past forty days! Let's wrap it up with a final prayer, followed by some food for thought to help launch you into a feasting life!

Jesus, I am hungry for the message of Your unending love. Since Your love knows no end, my pursuit of it will never end. I'm ready for a lifetime of feasting now! Jesus, it is in Your loving name I pray, Amen.

THE FEAST

2 Chronicles 30

FOOD FOR THOUGHT

If you do not yet have a Bible reading plan, it's time to make one! I've provided Bible reading calendars along with other downloadable resources to help you transition into a feasting life at wendyspeake.com/feast. They include:

- *Seven More Days.* Download seven more devotions! Today's passage of study inspired me to write seven more chapters!
- *Bible Reading Plans.* Choose from one of three different Bible reading plans. Print a copy for personal use or make multiple copies and invite your family and friends to join you as you journey through God's Word.
- *Topical Studies.* If you would like to begin by studying what the Bible has to say about a specific question or struggle you may have, a topical study is a great option. Topics range from anxiety and addiction to unforgiveness and the gospel message.
- *Bible Bookmarks to Help with Your Bible Reading.* Tuck the three simple questions into your Bible as you seek to understand God's Word in context, then apply it to the context of your life.

Acknowledgments

ONCE AGAIN, I could not have accomplished this work on my own. Though I labored alone for many hours over the course of a year, there were many who colabored with me. Any fruit that is harvested through the reading of this book is shared with those listed below. I am so grateful for each one of you.

To my husband, Matt, and our three sons, Caleb, Brody, and Asher: As I prepared this feast, I often left you to fend for yourselves in the kitchen. You ate sandwiches and frozen dinners so that others might learn to feast on God's Word. Consider this your formal invitation back to the table. As we gather around a scrumptious home-cooked meal, let's open God's Word together! That's always been my favorite family feast.

To my agent, Bill Jensen: You believed in this message more than any other person in my life. You cheered me on, sent pictures of pages out of books from your own library, suggested Scriptures and stories, and refused to let me shrink back from hard topics. I cannot imagine having done this without you.

To the incredible team at Baker Publishing Group: Your partnership in this trilogy of fasting and feasting books has been one of the great joys of my life.

And finally, to Jennifer McClure: You've been with me from the start of my fasting-to-feasting journey. While I dedicated this book to God in the opening pages, I want to close it out with sincere gratitude to *you*. This was the book you personally requested, emphatic that others needed it as well.

Notes

Day 2 Precious Moments

1. Charles Spurgeon, quoted in Nate Pickowicz, *How to Eat Your Bible: A Simple Approach to Learning and Loving the Word of God* (Chicago: Moody Publishers, 2021), 35–36.

Day 4 Torah

1. Rabbi Daniel Kohn, "The Torah Service," My Jewish Learning, accessed May 20, 2022, https://www.myjewishlearning.com/article/the-torah-service/.
2. Tzvi Freeman, "What Is Torah?," Chabad.org, accessed May 20, 2022, https://www.chabad.org/library/article_cdo/aid/1426382/jewish/Torah.htm.
3. Corrie ten Boom, quoted in Carol McLeod, *StormProof: Weathering Life's Tough Times* (New Kensington, PA: Whitaker House, 2019), 161.

Day 5 Transforming Still

1. H. A. Ironside, *Random Reminiscences from Fifty Years of Ministry* (New York: Loizeaux Brothers, 1939; CrossReach Publications, 2017), 51–53.
2. Ironside, *Random Reminiscences*, 51–53.
3. Attributed to D. L. Moody in Ken Harrison, *Rise of the Servant Kings: What the Bible Says about Being a Man* (Colorado Springs: Multnomah, 2020), 49.

Day 6 Why, Not How

1. Sally Lloyd-Jones, *The Jesus Storybook Bible* (Grand Rapids: ZonderKids, 2007), 16.
2. James Merritt, quoted in Randy Alcorn, *Truth: A Bigger View of God's Word* (Eugene, OR: Harvest House Publishers, 2017), 144.

Day 7 The Word Made Flesh

1. "What Does It Mean That the Word became Flesh (John 1:14)?," Got Questions, accessed May 12, 2022, https://www.gotquestions.org/Word-became-flesh .html.

Day 8 Bible Wounds

1. Charles H. Spurgeon, "Christ's Hospital: A Sermon on Psalm 147:3," originally published in *Metropolitan Tabernacle Pulpit*, vol. 38 (1892).

2. "Zacchaeus Was a Wee Little Man," Genius, accessed July 19, 2022, https:// genius.com/Traditional-zacchaeus-was-a-wee-little-man-lyrics. Author unknown. Public domain.

Day 9 The Book That Understands Me

1. Emile Cailliet, *Journey into Light* (Grand Rapids: Zondervan, 1968), 16.

2. Cailliet's story is recounted in James Montgomery Boice, *Foundations of the Christian Faith: A Comprehensive and Readable Theology*, rev. and expanded ed. (Downers Grove, IL: InterVarsity Press, 1986, 2019), 38–39.

3. Cailliet, *Journey into Light*, 11–18.

Day 11 Our Daily Bread

1. "*Daily Light on the Daily Path* and the Bagster Family," Wholesome Words, 2012, accessed May 20, 2022, https://www.wholesomewords.org/resources/bbag ster.html.

Day 12 Thy Word

1. C. Michael Hawn, "History of Hymns: Praise Chorus Affirms Jesus as Guiding Light," Discipleship Ministries, United Methodist Church, May 21, 2013, https:// www.umcdiscipleship.org/resources/history-of-hymns-praise-chorus-affirms -jesus-as-guiding-light.

2. C. Michael Hawn, "History of Hymns: 'Trust and Obey,'" Discipleship Ministries, United Methodist Church, June 20, 2013, https://www.umcdiscipleship.org /resources/history-of-hymns-trust-and-obey.

3. John H. Sammis, "When We Walk with the Lord," *The Covenant Hymnal* (Chicago: Covenant Publications, 1996), 376.

Day 13 Thirsty

1. C. Michael Hawn, "History of Hymns: 'As the Deer,'" Discipleship Ministries, United Methodist Church, November 13, 2014, https://www.umcdiscipleship.org /resources/history-of-hymns-as-the-deer.

2. Martin Nystrom, "As the Deer," (Brentwood, TN: Universal Music, Brentwood-Benson Publishing, 1984).

3. A. W. Tozer, *The Pursuit of God* (Ventura, CA: Regal, 1948, 2013), 28.

Day 14 Dry Bones

1. John Bunyan, *Grace Abounding to the Chief of Sinners* (Glasgow, Scotland: Porteous and Hislop, 1863), 132–33.

Day 15 A Firm Foundation

1. Martin Luther, "God's Unchanging Word," *742 Heartwarming Poems*, John R. Rice, ed. (Murfreesboro, TN: Sword of the Lord Publishers, 1964), 12.

Day 16 Did You Come to Hear from the Lord?

1. Matt Smethhurst, *Before You Open Your Bible: Nine Heart Postures for Approaching God's Word* (Leyland, England: 10Publishing, 2019), 6.

Day 17 Learning to Feast

1. Asheritah Ciuciu, *Bible and Breakfast: 31 Mornings with Jesus—Feeding Our Bodies and Souls Together* (Chicago: Moody Publishers, 2019), 23–25.
2. Sammis, "When We Walk with the Lord."

Day 19 God-Breathed

1. James Montgomery Boice, *Foundations of the Christian Faith*, 36.
2. "*Theopneustos*," Bible Hub, https://biblehub.com/greek/2315.htm.
3. FIRM Staff, "The Hebrew Word *Ruach* and God's Breath in Our Lungs," Fellowship of Israel Related Ministries, June 12, 2021, https://firmisrael.org/learn/the-hebrew-word-ruach-and-gods-breath-in-our-lungs/.
4. Bryan and Katie Torwalt, "Holy Spirit," Jesus Culture Music (Brentwood, TN: Sparrow Records, 2011).

Day 21 Inquisitive

1. "Inductive Bible Study," Seedbed, accessed June 23, 2022, https://seedbed.com/inductive-bible-study-history/.
2. Kay Arthur, David Arthur, and Pete De Lacy, *How to Study Your Bible: Discover the Life-Changing Approach to God's Word* (Eugene, OR: Harvest House, 1994, 2010), 11.
3. Tara-Leigh Cobble, *The Bible Recap: A One-Year Guide to Reading and Understanding the Entire Bible* (Bloomington, MN: Bethany House Publishers, 2020), 12.

Day 23 [Insert Your Name Here]

1. Wendy Speake, "[Hey Mom] Scriptures For Moms, From God," webpage, accessed June 7, 2022, https://www.wendyspeake.com/blog/hey-mom-series. Tweaked from original.
2. If you need encouragement in gentle parenting, I invite you to grab a copy of the book I cowrote with Amber Lia, *Triggers: Exchanging Parents' Angry Reactions*

for Gentle, Biblical Responses. Together, we can apply God's Word to that very specific area of your life.

3. Beth Moore, *Chasing Vines: Finding Your Way to an Immensely Fruitful Life* (Carol Stream, IL: Tyndale, 2020), 3.

Day 26 The Letters

1. Jim Custer and Tim Hosman, "I'll Obey," C. A. Music, Music Services, accessed July 19, 2022, https://musicservices.com/license/song/detail/44989.

2. Nate Pickowicz, *How to Eat Your Bible*, 19.

Day 27 Learn to Linger

1. Dale Reeves, "Chewing the Cud," Christ's Church, February 8, 2022, https://ourchristschurch.com/chewing-the-cud/.

2. David Mathis, *Habits of Grace: Enjoying Jesus through the Spiritual Disciplines* (Wheaton: Crossway, 2016), 45.

Day 28 Chew the Cud

1. Reeves, "Chewing the Cud."

2. Charles H. Spurgeon, *The Promises of God: A New Edition of the Classic Devotional Based on the English Standard Version*, rev. and updated by Tim Chester (Wheaton: Crossway, 2019), 2.

3. Timothy Keller with Kathy Keller, *The Songs of Jesus: A Year of Daily Devotions in the Psalms* (New York: Viking, 2015), 29.

Day 30 Hearing God's Voice

1. Justin Peters (@JustinPetersMin), "Want to hear God speak to you?," Twitter, May 12, 2017, https://twitter.com/justinpetersmin/status/863167957014163456?lang=en.

2. Mark Batterson, *Draw the Circle: The 40 Day Prayer Challenge* (Grand Rapids: Zondervan, 2012), 120.

Day 31 Talk with Your Mouth Full

1. Mark Batterson, endorsement for Jodi Berndt, *Praying the Scriptures for Your Life* (Grand Rapids: Zondervan, 2021), i.

2. Eugene H. Peterson, *Answering God: The Psalms as Tools for Prayer* (San Francisco: Harper & Row, 1989), 12, 86.

3. John Spurgeon, quoted in Jonathan Hayashi, "20 John Spurgeon Quotes that Changed My Life," Evangelica Sola, May 28, 2019, https://jonathanhayashi.com/20-charles-spurgeon-quotes-that-changed-my-life/.

4. Timothy Keller, *Prayer: Experiencing Awe and Intimacy with God* (New York: Penguin Press, 2014), 55, 56.

5. Dwight L. Moody, quoted in R. A. Torrey and Edward D. Andrews, *Deep Bible Study: The Importance and Value of Proper Bible Study*, updated and expanded ed. (Cambridge, OH: Christian Publishing House, 2016), 33.

Day 33 When the Bible Is Confusing

1. Robert Zemeckis, *Forrest Gump*, Paramount Pictures, 1994.

Day 34 On the Table

1. "The Biblical Feasts of Israel All Point to Jesus," One for Israel, September 3, 2020, https://www.oneforisrael.org/holidays/the-biblical-feasts-of-israel-all-point-to-jesus/; Jessie Blackman and Susha Roberts, "7 Feasts that Point to Christ," Wycliffe Bible Translators, accessed May 28, 2022, https://www.wycliffe.org/feast/7-feasts-that-point-to-christ.

Day 35 For One and All

1. "William Tyndale," *Encyclopedia Britannica*, October 2, 2021, https://www.britannica.com/biography/William-Tyndale.

2. John Foxe, *Foxe's Book of Martyrs* (Peabody, MA: Hendrickson Publishers, 2004), 225.

3. William Tyndale, *Doctrinal Treatises and Introductions to Different Portions of the Holy Scriptures* (Cambridge, England: The University Press, 1848), 135.

4. "William Tyndale," *Encyclopedia Britannica*.

5. William Tyndale, quoted in John Foxe, *Foxe's Book of Martyrs*, 233.

6. Christopher Daniell, "The Deaths of the Reformers," *Tyndale Society Journal*, no. 6 (February 1997), http://www.tyndale.org/tsj06/daniell.html.

7. Eugene Peterson, quoted in "What Is The Message," NavPress, accessed May 28, 2022, https://www.navpress.com/what-is-the-message.

Day 36 When Progressive Is Regressive

1. E. Paul Hovey, quoted in Martin H. Manser, *The Westminster Collection of Christian Quotations* (Louisville, KY: Westminster John Knox Press, 2001), 19.

2. Alisa Childers, *Another Gospel? A Lifelong Christian Seeks Truth in Response to Progressive Christianity* (Carol Stream, IL: Tyndale, 2020), 24, 76.

Wendy Speake is the author of *The 40-Day Sugar Fast*, *The 40-Day Social Media Fast*, and coauthor of the popular parenting book *Triggers: Exchanging Parents' Angry Reactions for Gentle Biblical Responses*. Wendy hosts her online 40-Day Sugar Fast every January. To find out more, visit wendyspeake.com.

Ready to Go — DEEPER?

Join the annual online 40-DAY SUGAR FAST.

Every January, author Wendy Speake leads a group of Jesus-hungry men and women through forty days of fasting from sugar in order to feast together on the satisfying sweetness of our Savior! Join the private Facebook group for a powerful and transformative experience.

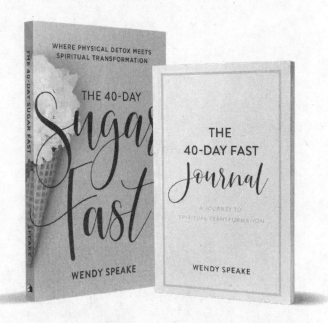

Visit **40daysugarfast.com**
to SIGN UP for our next community-wide fast.

Disconnect from Technology to
RECONNECT WITH GOD

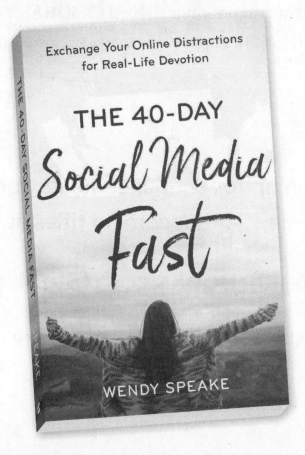

In the pattern of her popular book *The 40-Day Sugar Fast*, Wendy Speake offers you *The 40-Day Social Media Fast*. This "screen sabbatical" is designed to help you become fully conscious of your dependence on social media so you can purposefully unplug from screens and plug into real life with the help of a very real God.